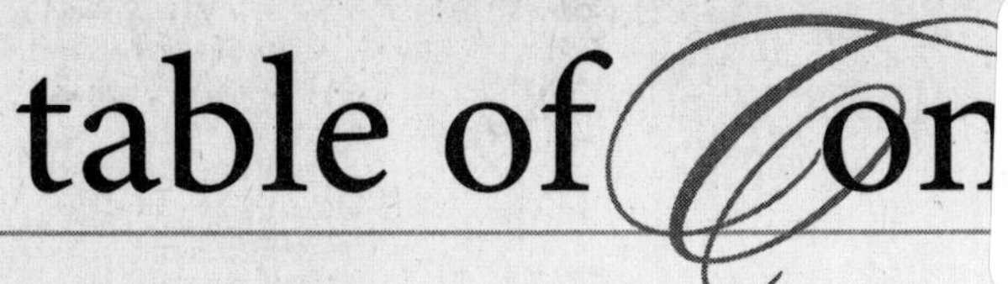

MW01623779

A Heart Like His

Welcome to this study of episodes from *A Heart Like His!* I am thrilled you've chosen to take this journey through Scripture with me! We have quite an expedition before us as we tour the pastures, caves, and palace of one of the most well-known figures in history—King David.

We will quickly discover David's multifaceted personality. Our responses to his experiences will likely be as diverse as he was. He will make us laugh, and he will make us cry. He will delight us, and he will disappoint us. He will make us want to be just like him at times and nothing like him at others. He is sure to capture your interest, if you let him. And God is sure to change your heart, if you let Him.

David lived thousands of years ago, yet he dealt with many of the issues that plague God's people today. If you've ever had doubts, fought temptations, battled personal inconsistencies, fallen into sin, suffered losses, or anguished over family problems, this Bible study is for you. If you haven't, you may need to check your pulse!

Beth Moore

ABOUT THE WRITERS

Beth Moore

has written numerous books and Bible studies that have been read by women of all ages, races, and denominations.

Beth's ministry is grounded in and fueled by her service at her home fellowship, Houston's First Baptist Church, where she teaches a 700-member Sunday School class. Beth and her husband, Keith, live in Houston, Texas.

BETH MOORE wrote the interactive learning activities for this study.

JOE BECKLER wrote the teaching plans this study. Joe holds a Master of Divinity degree from New Orleans Baptist Theological Seminary. Currently he is planting a church in Durango, Colorado. He enjoys participating in outdoor sports. Joe and Cheri also parent triplet sons.

ABOUT THIS STUDY

"A Heart Like His" focuses on lessons from the life of Israel's King David. To have a heart like God's, we need to set goals for our lives. Look up the Bible verses and fill in the blanks as you set seven goals for this study and your life.

1-21-09 Days Inn Snow Day ☺

1. **A fresh** Knowledge **of God's authority (Jer. 10:23).**
2. **A deepened** Communication **with God through** prayer **(1 Sam. 1:27–2:1).**
3. **A ready __________ to authentic __________.**
4. **A reliable __________ of God's Word (1 Sam. 3:1,19-21).**
5. **A greater __________ to judge by appearances (1 Sam. 10:20-24).**
6. **A personal __________ to __________ and be restored (1 Sam. 12:20-24).**
7. **A heart __________ after His own (1 Sam. 13:11-14).**

master*Work*:
Essential Messages from God's Servants

- Designed for developing and maturing believers who desire to go deeper into the spiritual truths of God's Word.
- Ideal for many types of Bible study groups.
- A continuing series from leading Christian authors and their key messages.
- Based on LifeWay's well-known, interactive model for daily Bible study.
- The interspersed interactive personal learning activities **in bold type** are written by the writer identified on the Study Theme unit page.
- Teaching plans follow each lesson to help facilitators guide learners through lessons.
- Published quarterly.

Sowing Seeds of Jealousy

An Amazing Covenant

DIGITAL VIDEO

If you would be interested in hearing Beth Moore discuss the material in this *MasterWork* lesson for March 2—and more—go to *www.lifeway.com* and purchase your personal copy of "Sowing the Seeds of Jealousy," Beth's video for Session 2 of *A Heart Like His*.

When we open our study of episodes in the life of David, David already has been anointed king by Samuel, he has been playing the harp to comfort Saul's troubled spirit, and he has just killed the Philistine giant Goliath.

Read 1 Samuel 17:55–18:4. Describe in the margin Jonathan's feelings for David. Then describe David's feelings for Jonathan.

What belongings did Jonathan give to David in their covenant? ☐ bow ☐ turban ☐ tunic ☐ robe ☐ sword ☐ belt ☐ shield

Sometimes friendships bloom over months or years. Other times someone touches your heart almost instantly, and you seem to have known him or her forever.

Jonathan's expressions of love and friendship toward David paint one of the most beautiful portraits of a covenant in the Word of God.

What three elements accompanied the making of their covenant? 1.________ 2.________ 3.________

Jonathan demonstrated his covenant with David by giving him his robe, tunic, and weapons. We will see the significance of Jonathan's demonstration as we consider Jonathan's sacrifice and his solemn oath.

The Sacrifice

Jonathan was a prince and heir apparent to the throne. His father obviously planned for Jonathan to be the next king of Israel, but this son had other plans. In David, Jonathan saw character fit for a king. He was so determined that the throne be occupied by God's chosen instrument that he offered everything he had. In this unique covenant, Jonathan sacrificed himself. Jonathan removed his royal regalia—his robe and tunic—and placed it on David, symbolizing that David would be king instead of him. Can you picture the face of the recipient, whose clothing probably still carried the faint scent of sheep? Jonathan acknowledged David as prince of the Hebrew nation, a position that Jonathan could have jealously and vehemently claimed as his own. Men like Jonathan are a rarity.

Do you have the privilege of knowing someone like Jonathan? Do you know anyone who has given up power or position for God's will? ❑ Yes ❑ No If your answer is yes, briefly describe your example in the margin.

The Solemn Oath

The oath of Jonathan's covenant with David does not take place in words in chapter 18. However, it is symbolized in verse 4; then it is verbalized in 1 Samuel 20:13. Jonathan symbolized the solemn oath by giving David his weapons of protection: his sword, bow, and belt. He symbolically gave all he had to protect David from harm and insure his position as future king. Jonathan verbalized his solemn oath by pledging in 1 Samuel 20:13 to protect David from harm at great personal risk. Jonathan's covenant with David was based on Jonathan's love, not on David's response.

A Jealous Eye

In stark contrast to Jonathan's self-sacrifice and solemn allegiance, Saul regarded David as the ultimate threat. In our reading assignments today we will see a seed of jealousy planted deep within the soul of Saul. That seed will express itself with a vengeance over many chapters to come.

Read 1 Samuel 18:5-16.
What first incited the jealousy of King Saul?

____

How did Saul's inward jealousy become an outward violent expression?

____

According to verse 14, why was David a great success in everything he did? ____________________

Read the list of feelings below and cross out any that do not describe Saul's feelings in verses 5-16.

Admiration Jealousy Hatred Fear
Joy Gall Anger Anticipation Anxiety

I see at least four emotions attributed to Saul in his reactions to David. In verse 8 we see anger and gall, which ordinarily means bitterness. In verse 9 we see jealousy, and in verses 12 and 15 we see evidences of fear. When emotions are unchecked by the Holy Spirit, one negative emotion can easily feed another, joining together as links in a chain of bondage. The original Hebrew word for the kind of anger Saul experienced is *charah*—which means to burn, to be kindled, to be incensed. *Charah* points to the fire or heat of the anger just after it has been ignited. *Charah* captures the moment a person explodes with anger—the moment anger is ignited before any sense of control takes over, before a rational thought can be processed.

When was the last time you exploded over something? Go ahead and record it in the margin.

Did you have any regrets later? ❑ Yes ❑ No
If so, describe them in the margin.

Rarely do we accomplish anything profitable at the moment we become angry. Actions or words immediately following the ignition of anger are almost always regrettable.

Saul felt many things toward David, but the most consistent emotion was jealousy. Few experiences are more miserable than being the subject of someone's unleashed jealousy. Perhaps the only thing worse is being the one in whom the jealousy rages.

If you are the innocent subject of someone's unchecked jealousy—in the workplace, at church, in a relationship—tell God on him or her! Let God work! Pray for God to deliver you, to sow peace in your persecutor's heart, and to move mightily in spite of the wrongful response of another. If you are a sower of jealousy in your own heart, I tenderly urge you to ask God right now to release you from its bondage and fill you with His Spirit.

Read 1 Samuel 18:17-30. Why was Saul pleased that his daughter was in love with David, and what does his attitude tell you about his heart? Hoped he'd serve in war + be killed.

Wanted David's indebtedness.

Why do you think Saul became more afraid once he realized his daughter loved David?

Being replaced.

We know little about Michal, but Saul considered the marriage a way to destroy David (v. 21). Can you imagine the evil in the heart of a man who would use his own daughter as a pawn in a personal vendetta against someone else? Saul had high hopes that Michal would be the death of David, but David had something much greater than high hopes. He had a Most High God.

day Three

The Great Escape

Read 1 Samuel 19:1-18. In what ways did Jonathan respond to his father's orders to kill David?

- ☐ **He warned David of his father's intentions.**
- ☐ **He pretended to follow his father's instructions.**
- ☐ **He reminded his father David how had benefited him.**
- ☐ **He broke his covenant with David to honor his father.**

What was the result of Jonathan's efforts in David's behalf? Choose one.

- ☐ **Saul regarded Jonathan as a traitor.**
- ☐ **Saul's anger toward David deepened.**
- ☐ **Saul and David were briefly reconciled.**
- ☐ **An evil spirit struck Saul.**

How did Michal demonstrate her love for David?

____

In verse 17 what excuse did Michal give her father for deceiving him?

____

Today we will continue to see the power of jealousy contrasted with the power of love and the Spirit.

First consider how Saul's jealousy continued to grow. Jonathan was momentarily able to bring his father back to reality. He tried to convince Saul that David had been good for him and for the kingdom. Jonathan reminded Saul that he had initially been glad over David's victory.

Keep in mind that Jonathan risked his own life in keeping the covenant with David. Saul did not hesitate to order Jonathan's death once before. If Saul's men had not talked him into being rational, he would have killed his own son (see 1 Sam. 14:43-45). Well-chosen words calmed Saul's jealous rage, but it returned with a vengeance. Without God's intervention, we can offer only a small bandage to someone hemorrhaging from uncontrolled emotions. We may bring calm for a moment, but our efforts will have little lasting effect.

Have you ever been talked out of a negative spiral of emotions only to be captivated by those feelings again? If so, describe the situation in the margin.

We've probably all been in Saul's place at one time or another. Something makes us furious; then someone tries to "talk some sense into us." We feel a little better and pledge to put our anger away forever. Then, here it comes again with the power of gale-force winds. Our emotions negatively ignited can be more powerful than we are. Our best recourse when negative emotions begin controlling us is to fall before the throne of grace and seek God!

Jealousy is a powerful emotion, but so is love. Look back at 1 Samuel 18:28-29. Write in the margin why Saul had cause to be frightened when he realized Michal loved David?

Saul was right about love threatening his plans for Michal to bring harm to David. The power of love often exceeds the power of loyalty. Saul thought he could trust Michal to make David miserable. Saul thought she would be a puppet in his hands against the young warrior until he realized Michal loved David. Her masterful deception could easily have led to her death. Surely she was only spared because she convinced her father that David would have killed her if she hadn't let him get away.

First Samuel 19:18 ends with a vital piece of information. To whom did David run?

☐ Jonathan ☐ Jesse ☐ Samuel ☐ Eliab

Why do think he ran to this particular person?

God sent him.

Have you ever had a time in your life when someone encouraged you toward a position and once you got in the middle of it, you went back and said, "What have you gotten me into?" David went straight to Samuel because he was the one God used to anoint David as His chosen leader of Israel. David likely had questions for Samuel, such as, "Are you sure God told you to anoint me?" Regardless of his questions, David went to tell on Saul! Samuel received David and no doubt confirmed his calling.

Read 1 Samuel 19:19-24.

These events are almost humorous, aren't they? Saul sent one man after another to capture David, but every time they entered the presence of Samuel's prophets, the Spirit of God fell on them and they prophesied, too! Finally, Saul apparently thought, *Fine. I'll do it myself.* The same thing happened to him!

When God gets involved, we see real results. Don't miss celebrating that when a group of evil men met a group of godly men, godliness won. How encouraging to remember that the Spirit of God is more powerful than the spirit of wickedness!

Love is more powerful than jealousy, godliness is more powerful than wickedness, and the Spirit of God is more powerful than anything!

day Four

Sunday 1-25-09 SDSt [yesterday then to Athens]

Common Bonds, Uncommon Friends

As we find David caught in the whirlwind of Saul's jealousy, we also see this threat of death give way to the reaffirmation of Jonathan's covenant. Today we are going to talk about friendships, the "once-in-a-lifetime" kind.

In today's reading assignment, observe the relationship between Jonathan and David and the events that caused their separation.

Read 1 Samuel 20:1-42. Why did David flee to Jonathan? ____________________

In the margin, offer a few reasons why you believe David might have "wept the most."

In 1 Samuel 18:1-4 we studied the making of the covenant between Jonathan and David. Today we see the keeping of that covenant. Anyone can make a covenant, but only the faithful keep their covenants.

I have waited to emphasize a special portion of Scripture from our reading assignment on Day 1. First Samuel 20 poignantly pictures words so beautifully expressed in 1 Samuel 18:1. The Word of God tells us, "Jonathan became one in spirit with David, and he loved him as himself." The *King James Version* helps us draw a more vivid mental image: "the soul of Jonathan was knit with the soul of David." The original Hebrew word translated "knit" in the *King James Version* and "became one" in the *New International Version* is *qashar* which means "to tie … join together, knit."[1] Jonathan and David are examples of two people knit together by something more powerful than circumstances or preferences.

The Spirit of God sometimes cements two people together as part of His plan. God would never have chosen David to be His future king if He had not planned to sustain him and ultimately to deliver him safely to his throne. Jonathan was an important part of God's plan. They were un-common friends joined by a common bond—the Spirit of God. First Samuel 18:1 tells us Jonathan and David were united, but 1 Samuel 20 shows us!

Consider the tender expressions of uncommon friendship evidenced in today's reading assignment.

Uncommon friends can speak their minds without fear. Reread 1 Samuel 20:1-4 and imagine the tone David probably used with Jonathan. His words suggest nothing less than panic. Jonathan could easily have received David's words as an insult. After all, David practically took his frustration out on Jonathan and asked him to explain his father's actions. As you carefully consider the words they traded, you can almost hear their elevated and emotional tones. I believe as they exchanged heated words.

David came very close to holding Jonathan responsible for Saul's actions, and Jonathan came very close to getting defensive.

Their initial words to one another would be only natural under their circumstances. What is not natural, however, was their freedom to speak their minds to one another and move on to resolution without great incident. Notice that at this point Jonathan didn't believe that Saul was really trying to take David's life; yet he acknowledged that David's feelings were authentic. He didn't necessarily agree with David, but he agreed that David was upset and needed his help instead of his doubt.

Each of us can probably remember a time when someone has focused his or her frustrations on us and held us responsible for something beyond our control. How do you usually respond to this kind of scenario?

- ❑ **I ordinarily become a little defensive.**
- ❑ **I ordinarily become very defensive.**
- ❑ **I ordinarily allow the person to safely blow some steam.**
- ☒ **I ordinarily refuse to talk to him until he settles down.**

Uncommon friends can share their hearts without shame. The scene between Jonathan and David in 1 Samuel 20:41 touches my heart every time I read it. Something about two men unafraid to share their hearts with one another never fails to move me. Uncommon friends can be vulnerable with one another and still retain their dignity. The friendship between Jonathan and David was far more than emotion, and it was a safe place to trust and show feelings. They shared a common goal: the will of God. Each life complemented the other. They had separate lives but inseparable bonds.

Do you have a friend with whom you feel safe sharing your heart? ☒ **Yes** ❑ **No** **If your answer is no, and you wish you had an uncommon friend, use the margin to express a prayer for one.**

Uncommon friends can stay close even at a distance. Jonathan and David's friendship did not grow out of a lengthy period of time as most friendships do. They were brought together by spiritual ties, not sequences of time. They had "sworn friendship with each other in the name of the Lord" (v. 42). God brought them together. Their friendship was a bond of three.

Is God an active part of one of your friendships?
❑ Yes ❑ No If your answer is yes, indicate in the margin ways you and your friend keep God an active part of your friendship.

day *F*ive

The Blessed Reminder

Read 1 Samuel 21:1-9. When David resigned to live as a fugitive, he first went to Nob, to Ahimelech the priest, who reacted to David's arrival with trembling. Why do you think Ahimelech might have been frightened by David's coming? ____________________

What lie did David tell Ahimelech? ____________________

What two things did David request from the priest in these verses? ______________ ______________

The priest had no bread to offer David except the bread of ______________.

Who was Doeg the Edomite? ____________________

The only sword in Nob was the one that had belonged to ______________.

David did not haphazardly end up in Nob. David no doubt sought relief in the "city of priests." Nob, a village between Jerusalem and Gibeah, was the venue where the tabernacle was relocated after the destruction of Shiloh. Like many of us in times of crisis, David may have desired to draw closest to those who seem closest to God—not a bad idea.

Ahimelech "trembled" when he met David. Ahimelech was probably not aware of the warrant out for David's life. If he had known Saul was seeking to kill David, he would not have asked why David was alone. Perhaps verse 9 provides a little insight. Ahimelech knew of Goliath's demise at the hands of this young man. He also may have remembered David sporting through Jerusalem swinging Goliath's head in his hand. No doubt, David was rather intimidating. The priests certainly would have wanted no trouble from the Philistine army seeking revenge. Whatever the reasons, we are told that the sight of David struck fear in the priest's heart.

Surely you noted that David responded to the priest with a lie. Through our study we will be witness to more than a few compromises in David's character. In this case the compromise was David's willingness to lie. He was probably attempting to spare the priests' lives, hoping Saul would not hold Ahimelech responsible for helping David.

Famished from his flight, David asked the priest for bread. He asked for five loaves.

Read Leviticus 24:5-9. What did this bread represent?

Body of Christ

God reminded David of His presence, but David continued to run frantically from village to village. Surely Samuel reminded David of God's plan when David fled to Ramah. God reminded David of His presence and provision through the priest of Nob. God reminded David in another way too. Is it coincidental that the only weapon in the city of Nob was Goliath's? Is it possible God was trying to remind David that he had overcome a greater enemy than Saul with God's help? None of these reminders seemed to help, because David had forgotten to measure his obstacle against his God rather than against his own strength (as he had Goliath)!

---

[1] *The Complete Word Study Dictionary: Old Testament* (Chattanooga, TN: AMG Publishers, 1992), 105.

NOTES

Before the Session

1. Review news events during the week prior to this class discussion. Look for examples of loyalty as well as examples of jealously and disloyalty. Cut articles from the newspaper. Bring the examples of these news events to class. Either share what you discovered or allow learners to review the assorted articles. These articles can be utilized for the introduction discussion of Day 1 material.
2. A large volume of Scripture is explored in this week's lesson. As you prepare, determine how to best use key passages to emphasize the heart of the lesson.

During the Session

1. Ask: *With regard to news events from this past week, how does loyalty play into the events? How about disloyalty and jealously?* Allow learners to discuss the possible underlying emotions that affect news events such as the ones you reviewed as a class. Ask: *How about in our lives? How does a person's loyalty or disloyalty affect our attitudes?* Instruct learners to review 1 Samuel 17:55–18:4. Based on responses to the interactive activities on page 6 in Day 1, briefly summarize how Jonathan is portrayed. Follow up by asking learners to share how they responded to the interactive activity on page 7.
2. Read 1 Samuel 18:5-16. Say: *Compare and contrast this Scripture passage with what we just read about Jonathan.* Then ask: *What do you observe?* Invite learners to share how they responded to the interactive activities on the top of page 8. Ask: *How have you seen Saul's example reflected in people you interact with on a daily basis?* Refer to the interactive activities on the bottom of page 8 for further discussion. Do not pressure learners to share personal experiences, but allow several volunteers to give examples from their lives. Emphasize that our anger and jealousy can lead us to do awful things. Referencing 1 Samuel 18:17-30, explain that Saul chose to use his very own daughter to try to destroy David! Then discuss the interactive activities on page 9.

To the Leader:

David experienced the extreme loyalty of Jonathan and also the extreme jealousy of Saul. David's story is extremely relevant today because we too face the relational tensions of loyalty and jealousy. As you teach this lesson, create opportunities for learners to share how they deal with loyalty (or the lack of) in their day-to-day interactions.

NOTES

3. Review the events of 1 Samuel 19:1-18 with learners. Ask learners to share their responses to the interactive activities on page 10. Ask: *Who in your life has stood up for you? How did this person (or group of people) help you?* Emphasize that Saul was unstable. Even with the petitions of his own children, Saul went from one emotion to another. This was difficult for David. Ask: *How do you typically deal with people who swing from one emotion to another?* Refer to the interactive activity on the top of page 11 for further discussion. Emphasize that jealously is dangerous. It destroyed Saul. Yet love and loyalty are stronger. Refer to the events mentioned in 1 Samuel 18:28-29 and 19:19-24 and to the material on pages 11-12 to emphasize this truth.
4. Ask: *What words would you use to describe Jonathan?* Summarize the account in 1 Samuel 20:1-42. Explain that often we go through life without enjoying the type of friendship Jonathan and David enjoyed. Review with learners the three qualities of friendship displayed by David and Jonathan on pages 13-15. As you review the three characteristics, allow learners time to reflect on their responses to the interactive activities in Day 4. Then refer to the last interactive of Day 4 on the top of page 15. Ask learners to share how they responded.
5. Ask: *How do you think David felt after leaving Jonathan?* Explain that David had to live as a "man on the run." Life went from tough to tougher! Ask: *What happens to your faith when you feel like things go from bad to worse?* Read 1 Samuel 21:1-9 and review the interactive activities on page 15. Ask: *Why did David choose Nob as his place of initial refuge?* Explain that David knew that God was his true refuge and that Nob, being a town of priests, would be a logical place to go. Ask: *When things go bad in your life, is your first reaction to trust in God? Why or why not?* David needed reminders that God was on his side. He was surrounded with reminders that God was present in his struggle, namely the sword of Goliath and the bread of the presence. Explain that the show bread was a representation of God's presence (see Lev. 24:5-9).
6. Even with the reminders God gave David in the city of Nob, David still struggled to trust in God. Conclude this lesson by asking: *Where in your life right now is it most difficult to trust God?* Allow time for responses. Use learners' responses to pray for them in a closing prayer.

Tragic Ends and Faithful Friends

A Case of Overkill

Read 1 Samuel 27. The Philistines had been one of the greatest foes of the Israelites. In the margin, suggest why David and his 600 men settled in the Philistines area.

In response to David's request, Achish gave him the town of Ziklag for his settlement. How long did David remain in Philistine territory? ______________

Did David's practice in the land of the Philistines seem excessive or uncharacteristic to you? ☐ Yes ☐ No If so, indicate how in the margin.

In your own words, write in the margin what Achish said to himself about David.

My mind was filled with questions after first reading 1 Samuel 27. What has happened to David? Why was he taking up an alliance with the Philistines? Why was he on a rampage with every surrounding village? Did you have a few of the same questions? I believe two verses hold the keys for understanding David's uncharacteristic actions.

Reread verse 1. What had David concluded? ______________

Reread verse 11. What reason is given for David leaving no one alive? ______________________________

DIGITAL VIDEO

If you would be interested in hearing Beth Moore discuss the material in this *MasterWork* lesson for March 9—and more—go to *www.lifeway.com* and purchase your personal copy of "Tragic Ends and Faithful Friends," Beth's video for Session 4 of *A Heart Like His*.

Life on the run obviously took its toll. Fear, frustration, and exhaustion apparently caused David to experience hopelessness, perhaps even depression and panic. Possibly he was driven to the point of paranoia. The result was a literal case of overkill. You can hear the downward spiral of his mood as you look closely at the first verse of the chapter: "One of these days I will be destroyed by the hand of Saul."

David was facing what seemed to be the inevitable. Death appeared imminent. He was convinced he would ultimately be destroyed by the hands of a madman. He believed his only option was to escape to the land of the Philistines. He knew firsthand that Saul was scared of them. David surmised he would at least be safe for a while if he lived among the Philistines. He felt like giving up, but he couldn't because everyone had become an enemy in his eyes! Therefore, he fought everyone with a vengeance, with the exception of his two clear enemies: Saul and the Philistines. No doubt he was right to keep his hands off Saul, for he was the Lord's. We have no way of knowing how God responded to his alliance with the Philistines.

Look at a psalm scholars believe David penned at this time in his life. Perhaps we will gain some insight into the feelings he was experiencing. His feelings may have caused him to make either the wrong choices or the right choices for the wrong reasons.

Read Psalm 10. In the margin, record why you think David might have felt as if God were far away and hidden in times of trouble.

Which of the following words from verse 2 are ways David characterized his enemy?

☑ arrogant ☑ scheming ☑ dishonest ☐ mighty

In which of the following ways did David characterize himself, the victim?

☑ weak ☑ afraid ☑ sick ☑ grieved

Do you see what happens when we focus more on our battles than on God? Our enemy appears bigger, we appear weaker, and our God appears smaller. *Beware!* Long-term battle can cause vision impairment if eyes focus anywhere but up!

In your own words, what did David apparently believe Saul was saying to himself in verse 6? ____________

In your own words, what did David believe Saul was saying to himself in verse 11? ____________

Complete verse 13: "Why does the wicked man revile God? Why does he say to himself ____________ **?"**

What must the "victim" do according to verse 14?

____

According to verse 17, what three actions does God take in behalf of His children?

____

David's most obvious problem was that he felt so powerless and out of control in one area that he wielded an inappropriate amount of power and control in another.

The Living Dead

Today we are going to study a very peculiar encounter in Scripture and one without precedent. We may share some puzzling moments, some difficult moments, and some humorous moments. God is sovereign. He is Lord over the living and the dead.

Read 1 Samuel 28. Record the action Saul had previously taken according to verse 3. EXPELLED Mediums from Land.

When the Lord did not answer Saul by "dreams or Urim or prophets," what did he ask his attendants to do? FIND A MEDIUM.

What did Saul want the woman from Endor to do for him? Reach Samuel

Why do you think the woman cried out at the top of her voice when she saw Samuel? Saul was there

In what ways did the woman at Endor describe the man in the vision, convincing Saul it was Samuel?

Robe, old

According to the prophet Samuel, why did God refuse to answer Saul? Saul had turned away

What two prophecies did Samuel issue to Saul?

Lose Israel + his sons.

Unconfessed, unrepented sin can easily be the reason for God's silence in our lives. Remember, Saul continued in disobedience to God. He relentlessly sought the life of an innocent man and even attempted to spear his own son! He had the priests of the Lord slaughtered and gave approval to an entire town being wiped out. He expressed some regrets, but he never truly turned from wickedness to righteousness.

Isn't it interesting that Saul set out on a journey to seek that which he himself had expelled from the midst of Israel? He certainly didn't have a difficult time finding a spiritist either, suggesting that when we don't take God too seriously, others don't take our leadership too seriously!

In the margin record what Deuteronomy 18:10-12 says about spiritists and mediums.

Saul knew God's Word. Early in his reign as king he did what God's Word commanded. After his regard for God shrunk and his flesh abounded, he sought the very thing he once had considered wrong. We've done the same from time to time. We've felt convicted to get rid of something or to cease a certain practice; then, when our regard for God began to shrink and our regard for our own flesh began to grow, we were out the door hunting it down. Can you think of a few personal examples?

No doubt, God had His own agenda the day Saul sought the witch of Endor. You almost have to chuckle as the witch almost jumped out of her skin at the sight of Samuel!

Neither Samuel's clothing nor his mood had changed. "Why have you disturbed me by bringing me up?" I didn't get the feeling this was a joyful reunion, did you? I think what Samuel wanted to say was, *"Now what?"*

We arrive at God's sovereign purpose for supernaturally intervening. The encounter ends with the harsh news of the imminent death of Saul and his sons. When Samuel said, "Tomorrow you and your sons will be with me," we do not know what Samuel meant. He may simply have meant, "You are about to die." Or he may have meant Saul and his sons would join Samuel among the redeemed. I'd like to think Saul and his sons took the opportunity to settle business with God, knowing of their imminent demise. Sometimes the most merciful thing God can do in a rebellious person's life is let him know he is going to die so he can beg for God's mercy.

Alone With God

Today our emphasis switches from Saul back to David. When we last saw David, he had entered an alliance with Achish, a Philistine and the son of the king of Gath.

Read 1 Samuel 29:1–30:6. Write in the margin the two arguments the Philistine commanders made against David to keep him out of battle.

David and his men returned to Ziklag after a three-day journey. What did they discover when they reached their destination? ____________________

Describe the response of David and his men according to 1 Samuel 30:4. ____________________

Reread verse 6 carefully. Why would the men want to stone David? ____________________

This passage paints perfect portraits of human nature.

1. Hurting people often find someone to blame. When we've suffered a loss, just like David's men, we often look for stones to throw—and someone at whom to throw them. Notice that David also suffered the loss of his family. He did not know if he would ever see them again. He had taken many lives. I'm sure he assumed his enemy would not blink an eye at taking the lives of his wives and children. David cried the same tears the other men cried, but because they needed someone to blame, they focused their anger on him.

2. Nothing hurts more than our children in jeopardy. Many things hurt and cause us to search for stones to throw, but, as in verse 6, nothing has the potential to cause bitterness in spirit like matters involving our children. They are our Achilles' heel, aren't they? Someone can treat our child unfairly and we're ready to pounce. We almost can't help living by the philosophy: *If you want to make an enemy out of me, just mess with my kid.* Can you imagine how many poor decisions have been made when parents have hastily thrown the stones of retaliation in behalf of their children? We are so tempted to intervene. Sometimes intervention may be appropriate. But whether or not it's appropriate to get involved beyond the necessary emotional and spiritual support, *no stones are allowed.*

David's men ultimately arrived at a place of reason. They chose not to act at the peak of their emotions—a wise response for all of us.

3. Nothing helps more than finding strength in our God. Sometimes no one offers us encouragement or helps us find strength. We'd better be prepared at times to strengthen ourselves in the Lord. Knowing how to encourage ourselves in the Lord is essential. The *New International Version* says: "But David found strength in the Lord his God." Others can help and be encouraging, but this kind of strength comes only from the Lord.

Read 1 Samuel 30:7-31. How did David make the decision to pursue the captors? ______________________

Why did 200 men stay behind? __________________

What was the raiding party doing when David saw them? ______________________________________

How long did it take for David and his men to fight them? ______________________________________

When the victorious group returned, conflict erupted over the plunder. What was David's apparent reasoning why they must all "share alike"? _____________

Let's share a few words of application:

1. Assured victory does not mean easy wins. God told David in advance he would "certainly overtake them and succeed in the rescue" yet we see references to exhaustion (v. 10); hard work (v. 17); a nonstop, 24-hour battle (v. 17); and four hundred escapees (v. 7). God was absolutely true to His Word. The end was exactly as God had promised, but what we often don't count on is the *means.* God often gives us a victory that requires blood, sweat, and tears. Why? Because He is practical. When He can bring about a victory and strengthen and mature us all at the same time, He's likely to do it!

God revels in overcoming and undergirding all at once. You see, God's idea of victory has virtually nothing to do with *plunder.* It has to do with *people. What* comes out of a battle isn't nearly as important as *who* comes out of a battle. That day God not only worked a victory *through* David but He also worked one *in* David. The man after God's own heart came out of battle with grace and mercy and a little better grasp of God's sovereignty. God gave him the opportunity to participate firsthand in the fight.

2. We don't have to "win big" to win. No wholesale slaughter resulted. Quite the contrary, 400 men got away, yet God called it a victory! David could have been furious with himself because he let some guys get away. Instead, he chose to focus on the ones he brought home: their families, his family.

The Death of Israel's Giant

First Samuel 31:1 records the victory of the Philistines over Israel. Based on God's promise to Israel in Deuteronomy 11:22-25, why do you think Israel lost the battle? ____________________________________

What request did Saul make of his armor-bearer?

____

What was Saul's final action? ____________________

What did the Philistines do with Saul's body?_______

War is hard stuff, even when you're only a spectator.

Saul, critically wounded and hardly able to move, urged his armor-bearer to take his life. Saul knew the history of the Philistines. He knew they made sport of their prize captives. The armor-bearer must have stood frozen as he watched the wounded and bleeding king muster his last bit of strength to fall on his sword.

The Philistines did not need Saul alive to mock him. They cut off his head, surely in memory of their slain giant, and impaled his body on the wall of Beth Shan. The valiant men of Jabesh Gilead heard the news and removed the bodies and burned them.

The men of Jabesh Gilead performed a brave and loving act. Certainly the bodies were well-guarded. They could have ended up impaled beside the bodies they came to rescue. Why would they take such a chance?

Read 1 Samuel 11:1-11. Write in the margin why the people of Jabesh Gilead owed honor to Saul.

The men of Jabesh Gilead paid a tribute to a king who started well. They showed their gratitude, even after 40 years.

Is there anyone you've never thanked appropriately for kindness done in your behalf? ❑ Yes ❑ No If so, write in the margin how you could show your appreciation.

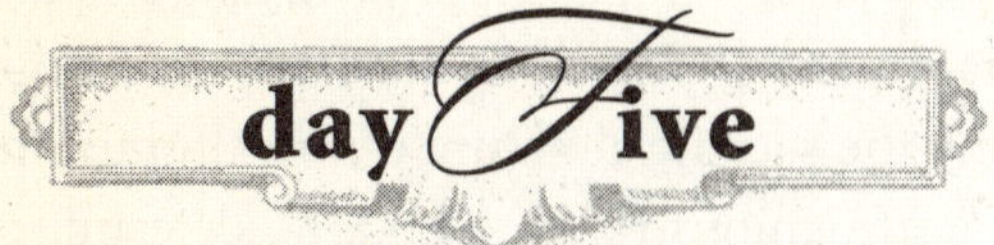

A Fallen Friend

Read 2 Samuel 1:1-16. According to verse 2, how long a period of time passed before David learned of Saul's death? ________________________

What lie did the Amalekite tell about Saul's death?

____

How did David and his men respond to the news about Saul and Jonathan? ________________________

Why do you think David had a unique right to ask the question in verse 14? ________________________

At least one opportunist was hoping he'd find favor with David by claiming he had taken the life of Saul. He was dead wrong.

Read 2 Samuel 1:17-27. In David's song of lament, why did he not want word of Saul's death and the deaths of his sons told in Gath and Ashkelon?

____

Describe in the margin David's apparent feelings toward Jonathan in his lament.

In David's song of lament, his words suddenly turn from the refrain of the assembly to the grief of a single heart. Using a term of affection, David cried, "I grieve for you, Jonathan, my brother."

David called his friend's love for him "wonderful." The Hebrew word for *wonderful* is *pala* (v. 26). It means "to be distinguished, to be astonishing, or to be extraordinary." Clearly, we see from the definition that David was distinguishing the sacrificial nature of this friendship from anything else anyone had ever demonstrated to him. So determined was Jonathan that David be king, a position which Jonathan stood to inherit, Jonathan committed his entire life to that end. David found it "astonishing."

David grieved the tragic loss of life that took place on Mount Gilboa. His thoughts must have been consumed with how differently he wished it had all happened.

Not coincidentally, 2 Samuel 2:1 begins with the words, "In the course of time." Some things such as grief just take "the course of time." Nothing else works. You can bet some lonely hours filled that "course of time." Some tears. Some regrets. Some endless replays. Some anger. Some confusion. But it did finally pass. Not the ache, but the pain. Blessedly, thankfully "in the course of time."

Have you ever experienced a loss only time could heal? ❑ Yes ❑ No If your answer is yes, how much time passed before you started to sense God's healing? ______________________________

NOTES

Before the Session

1. If possible, identify a learner in your class who has experienced a situation that brought chaos and confusion into his or her life. Prepare this person to share about that experience. In particular, allow the person to reflect on how the personal chaos affected his or her relationship with God and with other people.
2. Bring a set of cards or blocks to class. Before class, in an area that will not be disturbed, build a structure out of the cards or blocks. Make it tall enough so it can be knocked down as an illustration for class discussion. For added emphasis, place a note below the structure that says: "Fragile, do not disturb."
3. A large volume of Scripture is explored in this week's lesson. As you prepare, determine how to best use key passages to emphasized the focus of this lesson.

During the Session

1. Call on the person you pre-identified to share an experience of "chaos" [see "Before the Session," #1]. Allow that person to share his or her experience. After this individual has shared, refer to 1 Samuel 27. Allow learners time to briefly review this chapter. Ask: *Why did David behave the way he did in the territory of the Philistines? What is your reaction to David's behavior?* Refer to Psalm 10. Utilize the interactive activities on pages 20-21 to reflect on this psalm. Ask: *How does this psalm help us understand David's internal struggles? When you examine David's feelings, what resonates with your own experience with God?*
2. Refer to the card or block structure you built [see "Before the Session," #2]. Explain that we have issues and situations that are just as fragile as this structure of cards/blocks. Knock the cards/blocks over and explain that sometimes our bad decisions lead to a crash. Explain that this is exactly what happened to Saul. Ask learners to summarize the events of 1 Samuel 28. Allow time for them to look at the passage of Scripture and at their responses to the interactive activities on

To the Leader:

The lives of Saul and David are compared and contrasted in this week's lesson. While Saul spiraled out of control, David experienced his own spiral of chaos. Remember that learners are experiencing a variety of different struggles that leave them feeling their own spiral of chaos. See this week's lesson as an opportunity to help learners recognize how God interacts with us in the midst of our chaos.

NOTES

page 22. Ask: *What's the bottom line reason Saul chose to visit the spiritual medium from Endor?* Explain that Saul was desperate. He was insecure because God wasn't answering him. Say: *Describe a time when you felt like God wasn't listening. Did you make good or bad decisions?* Remind learners that Saul received bad news from the experience at Endor. Ask: *Do you agree with the conclusion of Day 2: "Sometimes the most merciful thing God can do in a rebellious person's life is let him know he is going to die so he can beg for God's mercy"? Why or why not?*

3. Using the material under Day 3, review the events of 1 Samuel 29:1–30:6. Ask learners to summarize what happened in these verses. Inquire: *Think about when David and his men returned to Ziklag. What would you have felt if you had been in David's shoes?* Explain to learners that we take for granted that fact that our society is as safe as it is. David lived in a "kill-or-be-killed" culture. Ask: *Have you been blamed for someone else's hurt? If so, what happened? How did David involve God in his situation?* Utilize the interactive activities on page 25 to review 1 Samuel 30:7-31. Ask: *What do these verses teach us concerning how to react when resolving conflicts and crises?*
4. Review the event under Day 4. Ask: *With reference to 1 Samuel 31, why do you think the Israelites lost the battle?* Encourage learners to incorporate Deuteronomy 11:22-25 into their response. [See the first interactive activity on p. 26.] Inform learners that this battle was a sad chapter in the history of Israel. Yet heroism still abounded. Ask: *What examples of heroism and kindness are found in this story?* Refer to the last interactive of Day 4 on page 27 for reflection.
5. Explain that David modeled a healthy sense of grief for his beloved friend and also for the king. Allow learners time to review the material under Day 5, or introduce this material to them. Ask: *With reference to 2 Samuel 1:17-27, how did David react to the deaths of Saul and Jonathan?* David was willing to get beyond himself and see the tragedy of the situation. Emphasize that we also must get beyond ourselves in order to mourn losses in a healthy way. As a final application point, discuss the last interactive of Day 5 on the bottom of page 28.
6. Close in prayer, asking God to help us live with our end in view and to be faithful to our life-long friends and their memories.

The Long-Awaited Throne

Settling Down

At least 15 years had passed since Samuel went to the home of Jesse and anointed his son, the young shepherd. As 2 Samuel 2 unfolds, David is 30 years old. Let's see what transpires "in the course of time."

Read 2 Samuel 2:1-7. Why did David go to Hebron?

____

Why did David send messengers to the men of Jabesh Gilead? ______________________________

How greatly we could profit if we would take to heart David's example in the first verse of today's study. David inquired of God before he took a single step forward in his inevitable journey to the throne. Did you notice that David kept asking until he had a specific answer from God? He did not want general directions. He wanted to know God's exact will for his life. David wasn't interested in simply getting to the throne. He wanted to get to the throne God's way.

When David inquired, God instructed him to go to Hebron. The region of Hebron has a very rich biblical history. It has been occupied almost continually since around 3300 B.C. Hebron is located in the hill country of Judah about 19 miles to the south of the city of Jerusalem. Some very important people and events are connected with Hebron.

David had been on the move constantly for years. The Word of God abiding in him had probably been his only comfort. After settling in

DIGITAL VIDEO

If you would be interested in hearing Beth Moore discuss the material in this *MasterWork* lesson for March 16—and more—go to *www.lifeway.com* and purchase your personal copy of "The Long Awaited Throne," Beth's video for Session 5 of *A Heart Like His.*

Hebron, "The men of Judah came … and there they anointed David king over the house of Judah" (v. 4). What a significant moment in the life of our subject! At last, his private anointing years earlier became public! He was anointed king over "the house of Judah," his first step to reigning as king over the entire nation of Israel.

David no doubt wished that God would have fast forwarded a few of his years of unrest, but he knew God's faithfulness would appear "in the course of time." From the moment David became king over the house of Judah, he began his official works of diplomacy. He applauded the men of Jabesh Gilead for their "kindness to Saul" (v. 5) and pledged his favor to them. But not all could be accomplished by words of diplomacy and pledges of protection. The entire nation of Israel would ultimately have to be under his authority. Much like Joshua, the land was to be David's, but he had to take some of it by force.

Things That Bring Change

The pacifist in me would like to skip the bloody details of the civil war in Israel. The Bible teacher in me knows we shouldn't. Old regimes rarely crumble without bloodshed. New regimes rarely arise without bloodshed. Rich history is written on the pages of 2 Samuel depicting the end of an old regime and the beginning of the new.

Read 2 Samuel 2:8–3:5. In the margin write the names of the characters you encountered in the passage. Note items of identifying information.

One of the most important names we've read today is Ish-Bosheth. You may have been surprised to see him identified as one of Saul's sons. He is not listed as one of Saul's sons in the beginning of Saul's reign in 1 Samuel 14:49, but he appears in a final list of sons in 1 Chronicles 8:33, indicating that he was born after Saul became king. Obviously Abner, commander of Israel's army, became the man in the power seat after Saul's death. He placed Ish-Bosheth (also called Esh-Baal), Saul's youngest son, in authority. We are told that he reigned for only two years. We will learn how his authority came to a sudden end.

Second Samuel 3:1 provides evidence that *time* plus *conflict* equals *change.* We are told that "the war ... lasted a long time. David grew stronger ... while the house of Saul grew weaker."

God obviously wanted us to learn from David's approach to warfare because He included so many of David's psalms addressing the subject, such as Psalm 20. This psalm, written by David, is dedicated to anyone facing a battle.

Read Psalm 20:1-9. Fill in the blank according to verse 1: "May the Lord ________________________ you when you are in distress."

What parallel can you draw between Psalm 20:6 and Romans 8:34? ________________________________

When we trust in the name of the Lord our God, what will be the ultimate results of our battles according to Psalm 20:8? ____________________________________

Fill in the blank according to Psalm 20:9: "Answer us when we ____________________________________."

Compare verses 1 and 9 of Psalm 20. God is so anxious to answer us when we are in distress, but an answer requires a plea for help. In other words, we must call out to Him in order for Him to answer us.

David continually called on God to fight his battles for him. Consequently, David always knew whose hand had brought the victory. The battles God allowed David to fight were means toward a divine end. We cannot pick fights or choose our own battles and expect God to get involved and fight for us. But when *God* ordains or permits our battles to be used to accomplish a divine end and *we* depend on God through every sweep of our sword, we *will* grow stronger instead of weaker.

Suspicious Minds

We learned on Day 1 that the house of Judah was first to anoint David as their ruler—a fitting union since David was from the tribe of Judah. Today we will get to know a little more intimately some of the historical figures you recorded in the margins.

Read 2 Samuel 3:6-21. Refresh your memory by identifying in the margin who Ish-Bosheth and Abner were.

The Bible offers no evidence to support Ish-Bosheth's accusation of Abner. Consider verses 6 and 7 carefully. Why do you think he might have made such an accusation? ______________________________

How did Abner respond to the accusation? ________

What one thing did David demand of Abner before making an agreement?______________________

Time and conflict forced a change once again. Ish-Bosheth, in contrast to David, was fighting a losing battle for at least two reasons: (1) He was fighting for a position God did not give him. (2) He did not call on the name of the Lord.

Ish-bosheth followed the sins of his father and became jealous and suspicious of someone who had been on his side. The accusations Ish-Bosheth made against Abner resulted in a complete transfer of loyalties. Abner defected and marched to the other side.

Read 2 Samuel 3:22-39. Joab, David's military commander, made an accusation against Abner behind his back. What do you think Joab was trying to accomplish?______________________________

What did Joab do? ________________________________

What insight did these verses offer you concerning David's heart? Record your thoughts in the margin.

Consider David's words in verse 39, "I am weak, and these sons of Zeruiah are too strong for me." I believe David may have been trying to say that in comparison they had a far greater appetite for violence and insatiable delight for blood than he did. They were ruthless. Why did David keep Joab aboard?

One reason is found in 1 Chronicles 2:16. What was David's relationship to Joab? ____________________

Read 2 Samuel 4:1-12. How did Mephibosheth become lame?____

What do you think Recab and Baanah were expecting from David?____________________________________

Record in the margin any additional insights about David's heart you can draw from these verses.

Violence breeds violence. No matter the country or corporation, when there is a power struggle the most important question seems to become, "Whose side are you on?" Every person seems to look out for his own neck and attempts to pitch his tent in the camp of the one who can do him the most good. Remember, God never comes to take sides. He comes to take over. Joab and Abner were both Israelites. So were Ish-Bosheth and his murderers. What a shame.

We're not likely to draw actual swords and thrust them into the bellies of our brothers and sisters in Christ, but how God must be grieved when we use the Sword of the Spirit to unnecessarily wound our brothers and sisters. The Word of God is to be used as a sword against the Evil One, not against our own brothers and sisters.

The Shepherd King

What an exciting day! David was about to experience the fulfillment of God's promise!

Read 2 Samuel 5:1-5. According to verse 1, who came to David at Hebron? ____________________

What did the elders of Israel do after David made a compact with them? ____________________

According to verse 2, what did God call David to do?

____

God often referred to Himself as a shepherd and His people as sheep. He also considered every earthly leader over His children to be a shepherd (see Ps. 78:52-53; 100:3; 119:176; Jer. 23:1).

We don't have the benefit of David's experience with real sheep, but God no doubt believed David's qualifications as a shepherd would enhance his leadership. We can certainly learn from David's example.

Read 2 Samuel 5:6-25. What attitude did the Jebusites display toward David? ____________________

What did David call his new residence? ____________

According to verse 10, why did David become "more and more powerful"? ____________________

Second Samuel 5:7 tells us "David captured the fortress of Zion, the City of David." As the city fell into his hands that day, the new shepherd-king must have thought about God, "You have been to me what these walls have been to this city. No other excuse exists for my safety or my success. You are my fortress."

I love verse 12: "And David knew that the Lord had established him as king over Israel and had exalted his kingdom for the sake of his people Israel." *David knew!* Many things must have confused David in his previous 15 years. So many things he did not know: *Why had God chosen him? Why did Saul turn on him? Why did Jonathan have to die? When would God's promise of the kingdom ever be fulfilled?* David did not know how he would ever live to be king. But when God handed over the most fortified city in all Israel to him and placed favor in the heart of the king of Tyre toward him, David *knew* the Lord had established him!

In confusing times, recounting what we know refreshes us. David still had many unanswered questions. He would never know for sure why God allowed certain things to happen, but he knew God had done exactly what He promised. You may never know why or how, but you can always know *Who* is faithful. Sometimes we stand to learn the most about God from the situations we understand the least.

Second Samuel 5:17-25 represents the fulfillment of God's promise to David concerning the Philistines as stated by Abner in 3:17-18. Strangely, David had come so far, yet he was back where he started. The hand that wrapped around his weapon as he waited for God's signal to overcome the Philistines looked far different from the hand that had searched for a smooth stone many years before. The first time he ever used his hands in battle was against the Philistines. Now he stood against them once more. To a man on the run, the Philistines had been a temporary refuge. They had taken advantage of his homeless estate by enjoying his strength. To a king on his rightful throne, they were clearly an enemy once more.

Turning Mourning into Dancing

Today we will gather with the Israelites on the city streets of Jerusalem as they celebrate the coming of their new king but not until we learn some difficult lessons. We will see that worship is not only the ultimate freedom and privilege but also an awesome endeavor to be taken seriously.

Read 2 Samuel 6:1-11. What did David and 30,000 men set out to do? ________________________________

According to verse 3, how did they transport the sacred vessel? ____________________________________

What were David and "the whole house of Israel" doing as the ark was being transported? __________

Scripture records two emotions David felt toward God after Uzzah was killed. What were they?
________________________ and ____________________

How could the ark have such devastating effects on Uzzah and such blessing on the household of Obed-Edom? Offer your thoughts in the margin.

Imagine becoming emotionally geared for a great celebration only to greet disaster instead. Uzzah's death would have been shocking under the most somber of circumstances, but can you imagine the shock in the midst of such celebration?

David felt anger and fear toward God, yet Scripture calls him "a man after God's own heart." I think one reason David remained a man after God's own heart was his unwillingness to turn from God, even when he felt negative emotions. David allowed his anger and fear to motivate him to seek more insight into the heart of God.

We should attempt to follow David's example by allowing our questions and confusion to motivate us to seek God. At first consideration, the account of Uzzah and the ark is hard to swallow. God almost seemed mean-spirited. In times like these, we find out whether we have based our faith on *who God is* or on *what He does.* Because His ways are higher than our ways, we cannot always comprehend what God is doing or why He makes certain decisions. When we sift His apparent activity through the standard of who He is, the fog begins to clear. Basing our faith on *who God is* rather than on *what He appears to be doing* is crucial to our spiritual health. Let's practice this approach and see if it works.

What is 2 Samuel 6:1-11 trying to tell us about who God is? In the margin record any words used to describe God.

God is not trying to tell us He is *harsh.* He's trying to tell us He is *holy.* The key to viewing the ark correctly is found in verse 2.

What do you learn about the ark from verse 2?______

____

Early in their history, God commanded the Israelites to build the ark of the covenant according to very specific directions. Then He said, "There, above the cover between the two cherubim that are over the ark of the Testimony, I will meet with you" (Ex. 25:22). The awesomeness, the holiness, the majesty of God dwelled right there, between the cherubim on that sacred ark! Until God was incarnate among men many centuries later in the person of Jesus Christ, the ark was the sacred center of God's glory and presence. To treat the ark inappropriately was to treat God inappropriately, not just because of what it was but because of who God is.

Now, based on *who God is,* can we draw any sound conclusions about what He was doing that day? I believe we can.

1. God was setting ground rules for a new regime. God was ushering in a new kingdom with a new king He had chosen to represent His heart. He dealt with the disrespect of man through many judges and the reign of a selfish king. With a new day dawning, God was demanding a new reverence.

2. God wanted His children to be different from the world. God would not accept attitudes and approaches from His children that were no different from the attitudes and approaches of the godless. Do you remember how they attempted to transport the ark? They attempted to transport the ark on a cart pulled by oxen. Some very important history is written in 1 Samuel 6, shedding a little light on what went wrong many years later.

The Philistines had captured the ark; then after being struck with plagues, they sought to return it.

Read 1 Samuel 6:7-8. How did the Philistines transport the ark? ________________________________

Do you see what Israel had done? They had copied the methods of the Philistines many years before when they returned the ark to the Israelites. How careful we must be not to think that God is less holy because others seem to get away with irreverence!

3. God wanted His kingdom to be established on His Word. The Israelites had not consulted God's commands for the ark's transportation.

Read the instructions they should have followed that day in Exodus 25:10-16 and Numbers 4:5,15. How was the ark supposed to have been transported? ________

God masterfully designed the transportation of His glory to literally rest on the shoulders of His revering priests, not on the backs of beasts.

4. God was teaching the relationship between blessing and reverence. God revealed the relationship between blessing and reverence through the effects of the ark on Obed-Edom and his household. God desires His presence and His glory to be a blessing, but reverence for Him is the necessary channel.

Read 2 Samuel 6:12-23. Record in the margin why you think David's attitude changed once he discovered God had blessed the household of Obed-Edom.

According to verse 13, what two things did they do differently as they transported the ark this time?

____________________ ____________________

Michal insulted David for dancing before the Lord. Has anyone ever made fun of you or insulted you because of your outward expressions of love for God?
❑ Yes ❑ No If yes, explain in the margin how you felt.

Second Samuel 6:12-23 offers us the opportunity to see that:

1. All worship is based on sacrifice. David's bold approach that day in Jerusalem could only have acceptably followed the shed blood of sacrifice. David offered a sin offering first. He was acknowledging his sin and asking God to grant him and his people forgiveness based on the blood of the sacrifice. David was not free to worship God acceptably until sacrifice had paved the way.

2. Worship with abandon is an intimate experience. We see David almost oblivious to everyone around him, totally liberated in the Spirit, dancing through the streets of Jerusalem "with all his might"! We don't see David practice such outward worship often. Usually his worship took the form of songs, words, and prayers, but this was a very special moment! The glory of God was born "in the city of David" that day!

Completely abandoned worship often is misunderstood. David went home to "bless his household," but he was met with ridicule and condemnation. He did not allow Michal to quench his spirit. He responded to her with the words, "It was before the Lord," and he resolved, "I will celebrate before the Lord." Can you almost hear him say, "How dare you! My worship was not for you; it was for the Lord!"

We would miss a blessing if we did not conclude today's lesson by turning to David's words in Psalm 30:11-12.

I'm not sure we will ever be released to fully "dance" before the Lord, until we've learned to wail. You'll never know the experience of being clothed with joy until you've allowed God to remove your sackcloth. Like David, you may be angry at God for taking the life of someone you cared for deeply. Perhaps you are still hurt and confused. We have no idea whether or not David ever fully understood Uzzah's death. We just know he was willing to wait, to study, to hear God's Word, and to approach Him again. *Then* came indescribable celebration. David may not have understood more about Uzzah's death, but he understood more about God, which made his loss more tolerable. God is not harsh; He is holy. He is not selfish; He is sovereign. He is not unfeeling; He is all-knowing. Like David, we need to come to know the Lord and respect Him, and like David, we will love Him more.

NOTES

To the Leader:

This week's lesson looks at David's embrace of the kingship, as well as the complications that came with his new role. This lesson can help learners think critically about how they work through difficult situations with people.

Before the Session

1. Bring 3-by-5-inch note cards for use in the discussion under Day 3.
2. A large volume of Scripture is explored in this week's lesson. As you prepare, determine how to best use key passages to emphasize the focus of this lesson.

During the Session

1. Read aloud 2 Samuel 2:1-7. Ask: *Based on everything David went through, what do you think he felt when he was crowned king? Put yourself in his shoes. What would you have felt?* Explain that sometimes we, like David, experience the benefits of settling into something for which we have worked hard to obtain. David navigated a tangled web of circumstances to eventually get to the point of kingship. Ask: *How did David act toward his fellow Israelites? Why?* Refer to the interactive activity on page 31 for discussion.
2. Use the first interactive of Day 2 to review what happened in 2 Samuel 2:8–3:5. Ask: *What is your gut reaction to battle scenes like this one found in 2 Samuel? How did David conduct himself in the midst of war?* Refer to the interactive activities on page 33 for further insight into the heart of David as far as his perspective in the midst of war. Ask: *What can we learn from David concerning our conduct in the conflicts we face in life?*
3. Ask learners to summarize what they discovered in reading through 2 Samuel 3–4 and in the material under Day 3. Utilize the interactive activities of Day 3 to facilitate this discussion. Ask: *How does the story of David, Abner, Joab, and the others mentioned relate to our interactions with people today?* As the Day 3 lesson explains, we may not face difficulties as violent as found in this story. Yet we face relational conflict with others that can get ugly and destructive. Challenge learners to consider one person with whom they need to find peace. Pass out the 3-by-5-inch note cards and ask learners to privately list the person's name on the card. Instruct learners to list on the other side of the card one to two ways peace can be brought into the broken relationship.

NOTES

4. Turning to the material for Day 4, ask: *What does it mean to call David a "shepherd king"?* Encourage learners to utilize 2 Samuel 5 (as well as other passages) to support their answer. Explain that David, as king, had a huge responsibility to protect a kingdom of people. God used David's background as a shepherd to set the tone of his leadership. Ask: *How often do we refer to world leaders as shepherds? Why do we or don't we do this?* Explain that God is the ultimate Shepherd, and Jesus modeled this in His life and ministry (see John 10:27). Ask: *Who has been a shepherd to you? How has this person specifically been a shepherd?*
5. In continuing the discussion of Day 4, read 2 Samuel 5:12. Ask: *Why is this verse significant?* Encourage learners to see that David, even though he faced plenty of uncertainty, had it set in his mind that God had established him as king. Ask: *What promises from God can we be certain of as we live our lives today?*
6. Utilizing the interactive activities on pages 38 through the top of page 40, review the events of 2 Samuel 6:1-11. Review comments under Day 5 to help learners understand David's reaction to Uzzah's death. Ask: *What is your emotional reaction to these events surrounding the ark? What do these verses teach us about God? In particular, what does David's display of emotions show us concerning how we should react to God when we are faced with perplexing situations?*
7. Briefly review 2 Samuel 6:12-23. Ask: *Thinking about all that David had been through, what was at the heart of David's worship?* If time permits, review the remaining interactive activities on the bottom of page 40. Ask: *How have you reacted when people scoff at your worship of God?* Conclude this lesson by pointing out the two worship observations mentioned at the end of Day 5 on page 41. Challenge learners to apply David's attitude of worship in their own lives, especially if life feels complicated and confusing to them. Emphasize that God will honor our worship.

David's Virtues

Humble Beginnings

DIGITAL VIDEO

If you would be interested in hearing Beth Moore discuss the material in this *MasterWork* lesson for March 23—and more—go to *www.lifeway.com* and purchase your personal copy of "A Man After God's Own Heart," Beth's video for Session 6 of *A Heart Like His.*

Read 2 Samuel 7:1-17. Fill in the blank according to verse 1: "The king was settled in his palace and the Lord had given him __________ from all his enemies."

What concern did David share with the prophet Nathan? ______________________________

We've all experienced a sudden bout of sober realization, times when we are horror struck by our own audacity. This was one of those times in the life of David. Life was calm. Enemies were subdued. Perhaps he was taking a load off, perched on his throne, when suddenly his eyes were unveiled to the splendor around him. The one who found refuge in a cave was now encased in a magnificent palace. He must have looked around and thought, *What's wrong with this picture?* He responded with shock: "Here I am, living in a palace of cedar, while the ark of God remains in a tent" (v. 2). Perhaps several virtues could be noted in David's sudden reaction to his surroundings, but let's not miss the virtue of humility. He summoned the prophet Nathan.

God issued several wonderful and significant promises through the prophet Nathan in verses 9-16. Some were to David personally. Others were to the nation of Israel as a whole, and several were to David's "offspring."

In the margin, record under three headings the promises to David, to Israel, and to David's offspring.

King David sought the counsel of Nathan, and in doing so revealed another important virtue: accountability. David did not consider himself to be above reproach or the need for advice. The statement David made to Nathan assumed the question, "What am I to do about the ark?" His sudden sense of audacity drew him to accountability.

Notice Nathan's initial response to David: "Whatever you have in mind, go ahead and do it, for the Lord is with you." I believe God used David's concern as a teaching tool for both David and Nathan. He taught both of them a gentle lesson on making assumptions. Perhaps we would be wise to heed as well. God was teaching an important lesson through each man.

- To David God said, "Don't assume that every bright and noble idea in a godly man's mind is of Me." Good ideas and God's ideas are often completely different.
- To Nathan God said, "Don't assume that a leader I have chosen is always right." The Lord can be "with" a man while a man can make a decision "without" God.

God's message to His new king was so rich, so revelational! He began with a gentle rebuke, one we must remember every time we have a good and noble idea: "Are you the one to build me a house to dwell in?" In other words, "David, have I appointed you to do that?" God reminded David that He is fully capable of appointing a servant for specific tasks. If we are seeking Him through prayer and Bible study, we will not likely miss His appointments. We need to wait on Him even when we have a great plan.

When we wait on God, He gives supernatural strength and accomplishes the inconceivable! Did you notice that God gave David the initial vision for the project (the temple) but his offspring were to build it? God can entrust a vision or an idea to us that may be ours to pray about and prepare for, but never to participate in directly.

The climactic point in God's message to David comes in verse 11. Allow me to paraphrase: "David, you won't build a house for Me. I'm going to build a house for you!" What overwhelming words! We want to do so many things for God; then they suddenly pale in comparison to the realization of all God wants to do for us! David discovered what we will often discover: You can't outgive God.

God drew His message to a close by issuing what is often called the Davidic Covenant. He issued His promise in the form of a declaration (vv. 11-16). Notice that the blessings and cursings of God on David's son might be conditional (v. 14), but God's kingdom covenant was completely unconditional. The covenant rested on God's faithfulness, not man's.

What could be better than being appointed to do a marvelous task for God? For me it would be for my child to do a marvelous task for God! I would happily forfeit participation in the great things of God for my children to inherit the opportunity! God finally assured David, if I may paraphrase again, "You have the right idea. It's just the wrong time. A house will be built for My name but not now, and not by you. Your son will build My house." If I had been David, I would have been unable to contain myself!

Compulsory Praise

Read 2 Samuel 7:18-29. Fill in the blank according to 2 Samuel 7:18: "Then King David went in and __________ __________ the Lord."

Have you ever responded like David? Have you experienced a time when someone told you something you knew was an answer from God, and you wanted to run as fast as you could and sit before Him? If so, write about it in the margin.

After saying, "Who am I … that you have brought me this far?" David said, "And as if this were not enough in your sight, O Sovereign Lord, you have also . . ." (v. 19). How like God to keep giving and giving! David was stunned by God's words of prophecy over his family. What more precious promise could God have given David than to assure him He would remain with his offspring long after David was gone? What peace we can have in knowing God will bless our children!

As if David was suddenly overcome, he broke out in compulsory praises! "How great you are, O Sovereign Lord!" Have you ever experienced David's kind of praise? At times our praises are planned. At times our praises, though unplanned, are as quiet in our spirits as a whisper—times when our spirits identify the goodness of God and we quietly, reverently acknowledge His worthiness. At other times praise is absolutely compulsory—times when we would burst if we did not praise; times when whispers are hard to contain; times when hands are difficult to stay; times when knees seem to bend by themselves; times when spirit, soul, and body join in compulsory harmony, *"How great You are, O Sovereign Lord, no one is like You!"*

Read verses 23-24. List in the margin every distinction David extolled about Israel in these two passages.

Israel—I love the sound of the syllables. I love their history. But most of all, I love their peculiarity. Their very identity was in their set-apartness. We often try so hard to blend in. We sometimes resent that God has ordained His people to seem strange to the rest of the world, yet so much of our identity is in our peculiarity!

According to verses 25 and 26, why did David want God to keep His promises? ____________________

I believe God deeply desires to purify all other motives of ambition in us except the ambition that God would use us to draw attention to Himself and His great name. Our human nature is self-serving and ambitious. Transferring personal ambitions to the ambition of God's exalted name and character is a direct result of the Spirit's influence.

Read verse 27 carefully. How do you think David found courage to offer God his prayer? ____________

I believe David was referring to his petition for God to establish the house of David forever. He never would have presumed to pray this prayer without first being told the will of God. David concluded his prayer with the words, "Now be pleased to bless this house." In other words, "Go ahead and do as You've so generously promised!" David was saying "Amen" to God's promises! David believed God, and he immediately began to pray in accordance and anticipation.

A Virtuous Man

We will return to the battlefield as the nation of Israel was once again established as a formidable power. When the dust of war settles, several important virtues of David will emerge.

Read 2 Samuel 8:1-18. Write in one sentence what you believe to be the point of this chapter.

____

David spared one-third of the Moabite army and left 100 of the Zobahite chariot horses mobile. Why do you think he left any alive? Offer your thoughts in the margin.

What did David do with all the gold and silver he acquired from the nations he subdued? ____________

Fill in the blank according to verse 13: "And David became ____________________ after he returned from striking down 18,000 Edomites in the Valley of Salt."

Describe in the margin David's leadership at this point in his reign.

Although our hearts may not be drawn to 2 Samuel 8, this chapter undoubtedly represents the zenith of David's career. God had given him success. David had it all: fame, fortune, power, and position. For just a little while, David handled the unabashed blessings of God with brilliant integrity. We can glean the following virtues from our reading today:

***1. A spirit of* cooperation.** In 2 Samuel 7:10-11 God had promised David that He would give the nation of Israel rest from her enemies. David did not sit on the throne and simply wait for God to fulfill His promise.

He obeyed God's beckoning to the battlefield to participate in the victory! When God assures us of a promise, He desires for us to respond by assuming a posture of cooperation in the fulfillment of that promise. The study of David's life inevitably invites the student to ask himself or herself some difficult questions.

Have you exhibited a spirit of cooperation with God recently? ❑ Yes ❑ No If your answer is yes, briefly explain in the margin.

Join me in asking God to make each of us keenly aware when we do not offer Him a spirit of cooperation.

***2. A ray of* hope.** David did not annihilate his enemy and simply leave the nations destroyed. First of all, he had not been told by God to do so. Second, I believe his God-given motive was to bring the other nations to a place of subservience rather than a place of nonexistence.

Compare 2 Samuel 8:2 with 8:6. How did the Moabites and the Arameans similarly respond to their defeat?

____

King David lived in a harsh and cruel time. That he would measure the people with a line and kill two-thirds of them naturally offends our modern sensibilities. What we remarkably do see is that David had a concern for the spiritual welfare of the nations. That concern was a giant step forward for a man of his day. David left a remnant among the nations. David exhibited *hope* for the nations to bend their knees to the King of all kings.

3. A literal* dedication *to God. At this point David had never confused the source of his strength. Any return from his feats he immediately dedicated to the Lord. If he was praised for his successes, he quickly gave the praise to God. If he was exalted for his successes, he lifted the name of God even higher. When he was surrounded by splendor, he wanted God to have something more splendid. When he returned with gold, silver, and bronze he dedicated them immediately to the Lord. The original Hebrew word for *dedicate* in this passage is *qadhash,* meaning "to hallow, dedicate, consecrate to God, declare as holy, treat as holy; to sanctify, purify, make clean; to be pure."

***4.* Justice *and* righteousness.** The definitive verse of 2 Samuel 8 says, "David reigned over all Israel, doing what was just and right for all his people" (v. 15).

Second Samuel 8:15 describes the moment when David most clearly and completely fulfilled his calling! When God called David a man after His own heart, He meant it literally. For a season, the kingdom of David reflected the kingdom of the supreme King of all kings yet to come—Jesus, the Christ, the sovereign Victorious! These were the glory days of David's kingdom. God had given him the keys to the kingdom: *justice* and *righteousness*—keys to a kingdom that will never end.

***5. The wisdom for* administration.** The wise king knew that growth meant a greater need for administration. As the chapter 8 concludes, we see one of the first orders of business: the delegation of authority and responsibility.

In the margin list the various positions David filled according to 2 Samuel 8:16-18. (Names are not necessary.)

A good administrator knows when and how to delegate!

Are you overloaded right now? ❑ Yes ❑ No
If your answer is yes, jot down in the margin some ways that you can delegate some responsibilities.

In the margin describe what stops you from delegating responsibilities.

Room in the Palace for More

Today we will have the pleasure of seeing a tender aspect of David's heart.

Read 2 Samuel 9:1-13. Read verse 1 carefully. List in the margin the emotions you think David might have been feeling that caused him to ask this question.

Whose kindness was David wanting to show according to verse 3? ______________________

How did Ziba describe the son of Jonathan? ________

What two ways did David want to show kindness to Mephibosheth for the sake of his father, Jonathan?
______________________ **and** ______________________

According to verse 8, what do you think Mephibosheth was feeling? ______________________

God had fulfilled Jonathan's wish and given David everything, but Jonathan wasn't there to share it with him. David sought the next best thing. Ziba, a servant of the house of Saul, told him about Jonathan's son Mephibosheth. Ziba's choice of words is interesting. "There is still a son of Jonathan," and in the next breath he uttered, "He is crippled in both feet." His choice of words and timing intimates he might have suspected the son's handicap to disqualify him from anything the king sought.

In the encounter between David and Mephibosheth we see several characteristics of God displayed. Consider with me the following virtues of God.

1. His loving-kindness. David was searching for someone of the house of Saul to whom he could show *God's* kindness, not his own (v. 3)!

2. His initiation of the relationship. "Where is he?" David inquired. Then he summoned Mephibosheth immediately. Note he did not seek David. David sought Mephibosheth! David was the king! What could he possibly have needed? He had everything! But he *wanted* someone to whom he could show God's kindness.

3. His complete acceptance. David did not hesitate when Ziba informed him of Mephibosheth's handicap. David summoned Mephibosheth exactly as he was.

4. His calming spirit. As Mephibosheth practically came crawling before the king, David exclaimed, "Mephibosheth!" He knew him by name. David's next words were, "Don't be afraid."

5. His delight in restoration. "I will restore to you all the land that belonged to your grandfather" (v. 7). David's first desire was to restore Mephibosheth. David knew about restoration. He penned the words, "He restores my soul" (Ps. 23:3). Perhaps the most grateful response we could ever offer God for our restoration is to help another be restored.

6. His desire for another son. Mephibosheth came stooped as a servant before the king. The king came before Mephibosheth to make him a son. He was family—invited to sit at the king's table to partake of his fellowship as one of his own! Imagine the sight when Mephibosheth first limped to the table set with sumptuous delights, surrounded by festive activity, and sat down, resting his crippled legs at the king's table!

Shunned Sympathy

Read 2 Samuel 10:1-19. Why did David want to show kindness to Hanun? ______________________

The Ammonite nobles led Hanun to believe David had sinister motives for sending his men. What do you think Hanun was trying to accomplish by treating David's men as he did? ______________________

Reconsider verses 9-12. In one word, how would you describe Joab's leadership? ______________________

Who joined the battle according to verse 17? ______

Believe it or not, the account of this raging battle is replete with many virtues of David. I would like to highlight three outstanding evidences of God's character at work in David.

1. An active sympathy for the suffering. David knew better than anyone that a crown did not make a person void of feelings and oblivious to losses. Even though Saul was not his father and had often treated him with malice, David had grieved Saul's death. Likewise Hanun was assuming the throne of the Ammonites, but at the cost of his father's life. David believed in showing kindness, especially to those who had shown kindness to him. If those who had been kind to David were not alive, he often sought their offspring so he could show kindness in return. He attempted such an act toward the incumbent king of Ammon, desiring to express heartfelt sympathy.

David's extension of sympathy was rejected by Hanun. The Ammonite nobles attempted to make the new king feel foolish for trusting David's motives. "Do you think David is honoring your father by sending men to you to express sympathy" (2 Sam. 10:3)? A possible paraphrase might be, "Are you some kind of gullible idiot?" Hanun responded by humiliating David's men. By cutting off their garments and half their beards, he was symbolically making them half the men they were.

2. A fierce protectiveness toward his own. David sent messengers to meet the men so they would not have to be publicly humiliated. In effect, he threw a cloak around their exposed bodies and formed a plan to spare their dignity. I'm not sure we can understand what this kind of humiliation meant to a Hebrew. The thought of being exposed in such a heartless manner would be humiliating to anyone, but to a Hebrew, such humiliation was virtually a fate worse than death. They were a very modest people. Their enemy preyed on one of their worst nightmares.

3. A vengeance toward the enemies of his people and the mockers of his mercy. David did not just formulate a plan to spare the dignity of his men. He took on their enemy himself.

Which of David's virtues has been most outstanding to you? Briefly explain why in the margin.

NOTES

To the Leader:

Sometimes the hardest time to be at our best is when life is going really good. In such times we can get lazy in our spiritual walk and lose sight of God's best for us. Use this lesson to help learners recognize how David made the best use of himself when he was at the height of his reign. Challenge learners to recognize how they can display God in the best of times, as well as the worst of times.

Before the Session

1. Bring enough paper to class so everyone can have one piece. Use this paper for the Day 2 application idea.
2. Bring markers suitable for a marker board (or for whatever is available in your class environment). The markers will be used for a final review of this week's lesson.
3. A large volume of Scripture is explored in this week's lesson. As you prepare, determine how to best use key passages to emphasized the focus of this lesson.

During the Session

1. Ask: *Based on your study of 2 Samuel 7:1-17 in Day 1, why do you think David felt compelled to build a house of worship for God?* Refer to David's situation and concerns as mentioned in Day 1. Ask: *Describe a time when you felt compelled to do something for God. Why did you feel this way?* Both Nathan and David thought God would want the "house" right away. This, however, wasn't the case. Ask: *Put yourself in David's shoes. How would you feel if God put a halt to the plans you had in mind for what you wanted to do for Him?* Explain that David's legacy turned out better than he expected—he passed the task along to his son Solomon, who built the temple.
2. Encourage learners to share what they wrote for the interactive activity on page 46. Ask learners to reflect on 2 Samuel 7:18-29. Utilize all the interactive activities of Day 2 to facilitate discussion. Ask: *When you review David's prayer, what catches your attention? When you think about prayer, how often does praise show up in your conversation with God?* Challenge learners to discover how to pray even if life seems to give no reason for praising God. Distribute the sheets of paper. Instruct learners to write a prayer of praise to God. Encourage learners to find a solitary moment later today to read to God the prayer they wrote.
3. Allow learners to share how they responded to the first interactive of Day 3 on page 48. Ask: *Based on Day 3's lesson, how did David*

NOTES

cooperate with God? What does it look like for you to cooperate with God? Explain that 2 Samuel 8 gives us the sense that David was at the height of his kingship. Encourage learners to share from their preparation how David ruled in this period (or be ready to enlighten the group concerning this matter). Ask: *What can we learn from David's leadership as we consider the way we lead and organize our own lives?* In discussing this question, consider referring to the last interactive questions of Day 3 on page 50 to facilitate further discussion.

4. Ask: *Based on 2 Samuel 9:1-13, why do you think David felt compelled to show kindness to Saul's family?* Utilize the interactive activities on page 51 to generate quick feedback. Ask: *Of the "virtues of God" listed in the Day 4 lesson, which is easiest for you to display toward those you need to restore? Which are the hardest?* Allow learners to share a time when they felt restored or when they were able to restore another person. Ask: *Who, right now, needs to feel the restoring hand of God through you?* Allow time for reflection and sharing.
5. After reviewing the events of 2 Samuel 10:1-5, explain that they were unexpected and sad. After all, David meant no harm, just compassion for Hanun's loss. Ask: *How have you reacted when another person rejected your expression of sympathy or compassion?* Allow learners to share their experiences. Briefly review the war events highlighted in Day 5 and in 2 Samuel 10:6-19. Then review the "three outstanding evidences of God's character at work in David." Conclude by allowing learners to share how they responded to the final interactive activity of Day 5 on page 53.
6. Review briefly with learners key attributes of David's character that showed up during the height of his reign as king. Using a marker board, list at least one attribute from each of the five lessons that reflects how David lived in relation to God and in relation to others. Ask: *Of all the attributes we see in David, which seems the most needed in your life?* Conclude the class with prayer, asking God to help learners align their hearts with the attributes of God that were so clearly displayed in David's life.

The Wages of Sin

Up on a Rooftop

DIGITAL VIDEO

If you would be interested in hearing Beth Moore discuss the material in this *MasterWork* lesson for March 30—and more—go to *www.lifeway.com* and purchase your personal copy of "The Wages of Sin," Beth's video for Session 7 of *A Heart Like His.*

Read 2 Samuel 11:1-5. What was David supposed to be doing in the spring? ________________

David's temptation turned into three specific actions recorded in verses 3 and 4. What are they?

1. ________________________

2. ________________________

3. ________________________

The sin between David and Bathsheba had numerous repercussions. What was the first result according to verse 5? ________________

Few things frighten me more than this testimony of David's life. We too could be persons of character and integrity and without apparent warning destroy our ministries and ourselves through the choice to gratify our sudden lusts. Like David, a few short verses could record the story of our downfall.

As you consider this story, don't be drawn into their sin by romantic—and false—notions. We cannot afford to justify their behavior through sympathy. In our culture we justify immoral behavior with the excuse that two people were "in love." David and Bathsheba were not in love. They simply chose to act in a dishonorable and destructive way. We could speculate that he was intoxicated by her beauty mixed with an opportunity to display his power. She may have been enamored with his wealth and prestige.

We may wish we could get everything we want. The gap between wanting and getting is where we must flex the muscle of self-control to protect ourselves. David had risen to a position where his every wish was someone else's command. He had ceased to hear a very important word—one without which integrity cannot be maintained. The word is *no.*

Have you recently had to say no to yourself for something you really wanted but knew you shouldn't have? ❑ Yes ❑ No How difficult is it for you to say no? _____

David, the man of God, the Lord's anointed, the one who enjoyed God's complete provision, took what did not belong to him and cast himself headlong into scandal. He believed his own cheating heart. We do not have the luxury of considering the events between David and Bathsheba a rarity. Unfortunately, many people of God allow their hearts to wander and fall into adultery. The threatened institution of marriage in our present society, inside the church and out, beckons us to confront the actions of King David. His actions can teach us not only how adultery can happen but how it can be avoided or prevented. How can we safeguard ourselves against falling to the same kinds of temptations? Let's consider a few places David went wrong.

1. He was in the wrong place at the wrong time. Notice the very first words of verse 1, "In the spring, at the time when kings go off to war." David had once been a very effective administrator and delegator; however, he had exceeded the wise bounds of delegation and left himself with little responsibility and idle hands. David should have been leading his troops just as the other kings were leading theirs. He was obviously restless. Second Samuel 11:2 says, "David got up from his bed." Sadly, David had delegated so much responsibility that he left himself open to boredom and temptation.

2. He failed to protect himself with a network of accountability. At one time he had been sensitive to the thought of offending God. He sought the counsel of prophets and allowed himself to be held accountable. We've reached a season in David's life when he was answering to no one, apparently not even God. All of us need to be surrounded by people who are invited to hold us accountable and question the questionable.

David grew accustomed to wanting and getting. What a dangerous habit! This time he went too far. He took something belonging to someone else, and no one called his hand on it. But God held him accountable!

3. He was lonely. He allowed himself to be placed so high on the throne that he found himself all alone.

Reread 2 Samuel 11:1-5 and note three progressive areas of sin.

Step 1: He sinned in thought. David saw the woman bathing and then concluded she was very beautiful. Sight turned into desire. The seed of sin was first sown in his mind as he tarried on the rooftop, just as the seed of sin is first sown in our minds.

Step 2: He sinned in word. If the sin of the mind is not confessed and repented, it virtually always gives birth to the next stage. The meditation of David's mind turned into the conversation of his mouth.

Think how often sin not squelched in the mind makes its way to the mouth. If we begin thinking about adultery and do not allow God to halt the thoughts, we'll start talking about it in one form or another just as David did. The talking invariably draws us closer to action. Temptations rarely go from the mind to the deed. The second stop is usually the mouth.

Step 3: He sinned in deed. David flirted with adultery in thought and word, stopping at neither venue to repent and ask God for help. Action followed. David committed adultery and set in motion a hurricane of repercussions.

Contrasts in Character

Read 2 Samuel 11:6-27. Why did David bring Uriah home? ______________________________

Have you ever felt someone was faking an interest in you for an ulterior motive? ❑ Yes ❑ No Suggest in the margin ways David probably was faking interest.

In 2 Samuel 11:1–17 a stark contrast becomes evident in the characters of Uriah and David. In the margin list as many evidences you can find of Uriah's strong character and David's flawed character.

How did David involve Joab in his grievous sin? ______

____

Consider the words of verse 25 and describe David's heart at this point. ______________________

Consider four evidences of David's faraway heart.

1. David resisted many opportunities to repent of his sin and lessen the charges against himself. Most of us have been carried away by an overwhelming and sudden craving of the flesh, but we've often cried out for help before sin was heaped on sin. Other times we've thrown ourselves into a revolving door of sin, just like David, and continued in a destructive cycle.

Describe in the margin how, after his sin with Bathsheba, David might have behaved with repentance and integrity.

In the margin suggest why you think David didn't stop and repent. You might consider answering from a personal standpoint by asking yourself, "Why have I not at times stopped and repented in the earlier stages of sin?"

After David committed the act of adultery, even though the consequences of the pregnancy were already at work, he could have fallen on his face before God, repented, asked for mercy, and begged God to help clean up the mess he had made. Throughout his encounters with Uriah, David had many opportunities to consider his actions and recant. He didn't.

2. David was unmoved by Uriah's integrity. David's faraway heart was unaffected by an encounter with authentic integrity. Uriah's integrity should have spurred such a sense of loss in David that he could not bear to remain so far from the Father.

3. David tried to cover his own sin. Most of us have tried to cover our sin at one time or another!

Have you ever gotten tangled in a web of sin while you tried to cover the first one? ❑ Yes ❑ No
In the margin identify the emotions you felt during this season of your life.

The word *covered* in Psalm 32:1 in the original Hebrew is *kasah* and it means "to cover, conceal, hide; to clothe; to forgive; to keep secret; to hide oneself, wrap oneself up." When we try desperately to cover up our sinful ways, we are bound for disaster as sin perpetuates. Only through repentance will God "cover" us and "clothe" us with His loving forgiveness. David was trying to cover his tracks. God wanted to cover his sins. The latter means life. The former means death—to something or someone.

4. ***David involved many others in his sin.*** Apparently David never stopped to consider the position in which he was placing others. We too can become so self-absorbed we do not care what we are asking from others. We can be unmoved by the compromises of others on our behalf. Intense selfishness accompanies a faraway heart.

In David's selfishness, he involved a servant in his plans; he invited Bathsheba to a season of guilt and grief; he attempted to entice Uriah to compromise his values; he involved Joab in his sin; and he had Uriah killed. Most importantly "the thing David had done displeased the Lord" (2 Sam. 11:27). Still he did not repent.

"You Are the Man!"

Read 2 Samuel 12:1-14. Indicate in the margin why you think Nathan used an analogy involving sheep.

What was David's response to Nathan's analogy?

____

At what point did David admit his sin? _____________

Nathan responded to David's confession with good news and bad news in verses 13 and 14.

The good news: ________________________________

The bad news: _________________________________

The scene unfolds with Nathan sent to confront David. Virtually a year had passed since David's initial sin with Bathsheba. We know the baby had already been born, but we do not know exactly how old he was. Why is the time so important? Because no sign of repentance had yet occurred!

David appeared to be moving on with his life as if nothing had happened, but how do you suppose his sin affected his relationship with God? David wrote exactly how he felt during his season of unrepentance. Take a moment to look at what David was going through during the course of that year, as recorded for us in Psalm 32:3-5.

Read Psalm 32:3-5. What obvious toll did David's unwillingness to repent have on him? _____________

I believe Psalm 32:3-5 describes a malady we might call *sin sickness.* It also teaches us an important truth. Spiritual illness (unrepentance) can lead to emotional illness (groaning all day, heaviness all night) and physical illness (bones wasted away, strength sapped).

When the prophet Nathan confronted David, he used a method any good preacher might have used. He used an illustration familiar to his hearer and then drove the illustration home with the Word of God. His method struck an immediate chord with David.

Sometimes the further we wander outside God's will, the more we judge others and the less we show mercy. David was ready to fine the man "four times over" and kill him—until he found out he was the man! What was God trying to accomplish? I believe He wanted David to recognize the *grace* of God in the midst of the grave consequences of his sin. God wanted David to recognize he deserved to die. God allowed David to sit as judge over his own life and pronounce a death sentence on himself so his Heavenly Father could grant him the undeserved gift of life. No doubt, David never forgot that moment.

God rebuked David through the prophet Nathan by saying in effect, "I anointed you, delivered you, gave you Saul's kingdom and all that belonged to him. If you had needed more, I would have given it. But you didn't ask me for things I longed to give to you. You took something that wasn't yours."

David, through his behavior, wounded the heart of God by despising His Word. The Hebrew word for *despised* is *bazah,* which means "to disesteem, to scorn." David's disesteem cost him dearly. As the chosen king of Israel, the man revered for having the hand of God on him, David was the most well-known, highly feared figure in the entire world. Through him God was *teaching* the nation Israel and the heathen nations about *Himself.* David's heinous, progressive sin did a terrible thing. The *King James Version* puts it this way: "By this deed thou hast given great occasion to the enemies of the Lord to blaspheme" (v. 14).

The original word for *blaspheme* is *na'ats* and it means "to revile, scorn, despise, reject; to condemn, to deride." It contains the idea of disdain for one who formerly received favorable attention and then rebelled. What other nations had seen in David caused them to cast their eyes on David's God. Though many had not turned to the God of Israel, He had captured their attention and respect. David's actions caused the nations to lose their respect for God.

Through David's victories, God taught something of Himself. Now, through David's failures, God would reveal something more of Himself. God's actions regarding David's sin teach the very foundation of all salvation—God will forgive the sinner, but He will still judge the sin.

Painful Pleas

Read 2 Samuel 12:15-25. In the margin list the ways David responded to his child's sudden illness.

Imagine yourself in David's position after his painful loss. Read his immediate responses in verse 20. Which response would have been most difficult for you and why? ___________________________

According to verse 23, what appeared to be David's sustaining belief through his grief? ___________

Describe God's attitude toward David and Bathsheba's second child. ___________________________

David had been warned his son would die, and still he "pleaded with God for the child" for seven days. When the child died, the servants were terrified David would do something desperate. They were stunned when David received the news, got up, washed his face, changed clothes, and went into the house of the Lord and worshiped.

Did David waste his time pleading with God over the life of the child? After all, God's message through Nathan was painfully clear.

David did not plead with God out of ignorance or naivete but out of his intimate knowledge of God. God does indeed hear our prayers and reserves the right to relent if the change does not compromise an eternal necessity.

But you may be thinking, *God did not do what David asked. David's prayers didn't change a thing. Where is grace? Where is mercy? What changed?* Let's consider a few of the things that changed.

1. David's painful pleas forced him back to a crucial place of depending on God. Somewhere along the line, David had mistaken the power of

God as his own. He had so often been told he could do anything that he started to believe it. God demands we depend on Him because only He can keep us safe. When we depend on Him, He takes care of us. When we seek security in other places, He is obligated to turn us back toward home. When we refuse the less painful nudgings of the Holy Spirit, we risk more drastic measures. Tragedy caused David to depend on God.

2. David's pleas would satisfy his spirit in the many months of mourning to come. As he grieved the loss, he needed to know he had done everything he could to prevent the child's death. David did not want his child to die because he did not ask God.

3. David's pleas ultimately ensured his survival through the tragedy he and his wife would suffer. David's pleas returned him to intimacy with God. The return positioned him to make it through such loss with victory and enabled him to comfort his grieving wife.

4. David's pleas touched the heart of God to respond. God loved this man—just as He loves us. The one He loves He must discipline (Heb. 12:6). But does God's heart ache as He disciplines? *Yes.* Beautiful evidence of the Father's tender heart toward David emerges in this tragic account. God could not give David what he asked because He had to perform an eternal work and teach an eternal lesson. But He did something else: "Then David comforted his wife Bathsheba, and he went to her and lay with her. She gave birth to a son, and they named him Solomon. The Lord loved him; and because the Lord loved him, he sent word through Nathan the prophet to name him Jedidiah" (2 Sam. 12:24-25).

Out of *grace* God removed the curse on the sinful union of David and Bathsheba. Their union had been wrong. Their motive was wrong. Even when David found out Bathsheba was pregnant, he tried to manipulate a way for her to stay out of his life. But now we see them drawn together by terrible tragedy. God removed the curse of their marriage and brought a child from their union. *Jedidiah* means "beloved of the Lord."

"The Lord loved him." And God loves you too. His chastisements can be painful, but God never turns His back on us. He will discipline us, but He will not forsake us. He will always seek to draw us back to a place where He can bless us once more.

No Relief Like Repentance

Somewhere between confronting sin and restoring fellowship must come the bridge between those two vital works—contrite confession. We have the blueprint for the bridge of confession fresh from the heart of a grieving king—Psalm 51.

In five words or less, what was David's theme in Psalm 51? ________________________________

David's sin had injured many people. Why do you think he said, "Against you, you only, have I sinned"?

____

Write in the margin the six requests David made of God in verses 10-12.

Why were the two results listed in verse 13 dependent on God's granting David's six requests?

____

This psalm invites the vilest of sinners to drink from the fountains of forgiveness. Consider these phrases from each of the first 13 verses.

Verse 1: "Have mercy upon me, O God." So great is David's need for cleansing, so urgent his plea, he began his prayer with no introduction and no high praises. David recognized that until he had expressed repentance, words would be wasted.

"According to your unfailing love; according to your great compassion." David knew his God was complex and multifaceted. In his history with God, David had called on His sovereignty, His might,

His deliverance, His intervention. But at this moment, David called on the God of love and compassion. Only on the basis of covenant love could David dare ask for mercy.

Verse 2: "Wash away all my iniquity and cleanse me from my sin." Don't miss the most important emphasis in this statement—the word *all.* What a wonderful word! God's mercy is enough to cover *all* our sins.

Verse 3: "For I know my transgressions." Psalm 51:3 proves David could not ignore his sins! Are you in David's position right now? Are you carrying the weight of past sin? Is the guilt and remorse more than you can bear? Do you have a sin you can't seem to give up? You can't live with it, but can't bring yourself to live without it? Satan screams: "To give it up will be far more painful than living with the guilt." Refuse to hear another of Satan's lies. The freedom of Christ is worth the surrender of absolutely anything! Relief, not remorse, awaits the repentant!

Verse 4: "Against you, you only have I sinned." For those of us who have known God and experienced God's presence, the biggest heartbreak over sin comes with the realization that we have offended Him. God takes our sin personally. When we leave sin unconfessed, we scoff at the cross.

Verse 5: "Surely I was sinful at birth." David recognized something of the depth of his inclination to sin. With a fresh sense of shock he seemed to be saying, "Sin is as much a part of me as the flesh and blood that makes up my body. It's my heritage! Oh, God, have mercy on me!"

Verse 6: "Surely you desire truth in the inner parts." God is our one and only source of transforming truth. Deep inside in the secret places we are most vulnerable to lies. Virtually every external sin results from the internal practice of believing a deceitful heart. *Only* God can sow truth in our hearts, only we can let Him. God can always be trusted to tell us the truth, but sometimes we don't want to hear the truth.

"You teach me wisdom in the inmost place." The inmost place is where experience turns into wisdom! Wisdom is knowledge applied. Knowledge stamped on the heart makes one wise.

Verse 7: "Cleanse me with hyssop." For the people of the Old Testament, hyssop carried a powerful ritual and symbolic message. See Exodus 12:22-23.

"Wash me and I will be whiter than snow." When I feel weighed down by sin and guilt, I feel spiritually dingy and dirty. The image of snow speaks volumes to me at those times. As a freshly forgiven sinner, I am whiter than snow! I am cleansed and forgiven and absolutely purified of sin.

Verse 8: "Let the bones you have crushed rejoice." This line is perhaps my favorite in Psalm 51. David mixed the pain of confessing and turning from sin with the pleasure of restored fellowship. God sometimes uses circumstances and discipline to figuratively break our legs from continuing on the path of sin. Only the repentant know what it's like to dance with joy and gladness on broken legs!

Verse 9: "Hide your face from my sins." With a sudden realization of his own depravity, David could not bear for God to look. He was filled with shame. Allowing God to open our eyes to sin is not only painful but also embarrassing! Once we look, we don't want God to look. We must accept the fact that He's already seen our sin, still loves us, and wants to forgive us.

Verse 10: "Create in me a pure heart." The Hebrew word for *create* is *bara.* Used in Genesis 1:1, it refers to an activity that can only be performed by God and describes entirely new productions. David was admitting his need for something only God could do. Pure hearts never come naturally. In fact, a pure human heart is perhaps God's most creative work!

Verse 11: "Do not ... take your Holy Spirit from me." To David, the removal of God's Spirit was a fate worse than death.

Verse 12: "Restore to me the joy of your salvation." Most of us have borrowed these precious words from time to time. Sometimes our prayers seem to go unanswered because in our misery we beg for our joy to be restored without the obedience of fully turning from our sin.

Nothing equals the moment you begin to sense the return of the joy of God's salvation, but we must have the willing spirit to cooperate in His marvelous work!

Verse 13: "Then I will teach transgressors your ways, and sinners will turn back to you." What happens after God has created a pure heart in a repentant sinner, renewed his spirit, and restored the joy of his salvation? No more willing and effective evangelist and teacher exists than one who is humbled, cleansed, renewed, and restored! God will never have to goad this person to witness. His or her life will have eternal impact.

NOTES

To the Leader:

David's story of sin reveals the fall of a godly man. It shows the crushing effect of one sin piled upon another. David's story is our story. Learners, no doubt, have felt the sting of sin personally and observed sin's impact in the lives of others. As you teach this lesson, avoid letting learners talk about "the other guy." Instead, emphasize how we each deal with our own sin. If necessary, put people at ease by emphasizing that we all struggle with sin and face the tough realities that David struggled with.

Before the Session

1. Prepare for using a marker board or tear paper for the compare and contrast exercise referenced in the discussion of Day 2 material.
2. A large volume of Scripture is explored in this week's lesson. As you prepare, determine how to best use key passages to emphasize the focus of this lesson.

During the Session

1. Review 2 Samuel 11:1-5 as a group. Use the Day 1 interactive activities on page 56 to facilitate a review of this passage. Challenge learners to compare and contrast David and Bathsheba's story with our modern day context. Ask: *What do you think was the key contributor to David's sin?* Explain that David's story reminds us that even the godliest folks can make fatal decisions. We are all vulnerable! Review the three ways David went wrong as listed on pages 57-58. Ask: *With reference to the three ways David went wrong, which of the three ways mentioned is most notorious in our context today? Why?*
2. Ask learners to share in summary the story regarding David and Uriah. Using the material from Day 2, compare and contrast the attitudes of David and Uriah. Using a marker board or two tear sheets, write out the observations learners share regarding these two men. As you discuss these two men, ask learners to draw specifically from their responses to the interactive exercise on the top of page 59. Ask: *How did David's attempt at covering up his sin affect his ability to make good decisions? How do our attempts to cover up sin affect our actions and capacities for living well?* Utilize the "four evidences of David's faraway heart" on pages 59-60 as a means to facilitate discussion of the above questions.
3. Ask learners to share how they responded to the interactive exercises from the bottom of page 60 through the top of page 61. Explain that we often fail to think about how David must have felt as he harbored his sin. Read Psalm 32:3-5. Ask: *Based on Psalm 32:3-5, how was David's life affected by the fact that he suppressed his guilt and sin?*

NOTES

What words would you use to describe a time in your life when you harbored sin? Explain that David's hidden sin was killing him internally. Emphasize that a lot of us live with hidden sin; it kills our spirits and abilities to enjoy God's presence. If sufficient time is available, assign learners to write their own poems of repentance of sin.

4. Ask: *What word would you use to describe the way God confronted David through Nathan the prophet? Do you think God's treatment of David would have been any different if he had confessed his sin earlier rather than later?* Conclude the discussion of Day 3's material by reading 2 Samuel 12:14. Explain that our sin does affect God—it hurts Him.
5. Ask: *What is your gut reaction to the news that the baby died?* Emphasize that the baby's death is disturbing. The disturbing nature of all the events between David and Bathsheba gives us a sick feeling in our stomachs. This is an example of how sin multiplies confusion, pain, and loss. Ask: *What strikes you the most about how David behaved in 2 Samuel 12:15-25?* Review the four ways David was changed, as listed in Day 4. Ask: *Which of the four changes best resonates with how you have felt when God was dealing with your sin?* Emphasize the fact that David accepted God's punishment and the consequences of his actions. Emphasize that one of the best things we can do when facing our sin is to embrace the punishment and willfully accept responsibility for our actions.
6. Allow learners time to share their responses to the first interactive activity of Day 5. Ask: *Based on Psalm 51, what are evidences a person is repentant?* Allow learners to share what they learned based on the exposition of the phrases of Psalm 51 in Day 5. If learners are hesitant to speak, be sure to explain the biblical phrases as broken down by Beth Moore. Ask: *Of all the statements made in Psalm 51, what is most meaningful to you and your experience with our forgiving God? Why?*
7. Close class discussion by appointing someone to read Psalm 51 aloud as a corporate prayer for the class.

The Unrelenting Sword

Family Secrets

DIGITAL VIDEO

If you would be interested in hearing Beth Moore discuss the material in this *MasterWork* lesson for April 6—and more—go to *www.lifeway.com* and purchase your personal copy of "The Unrelenting Sword," Beth's video for Session 8 of *A Heart Like His.*

In this week's lessons we have a sobering reminder—God is faithful even when His promise is judgment!

Read 2 Samuel 13:1-22. Identify in the margin David's children listed in verses 1 and 2 and any information you learn about them.

Why do you think Amnon's love turned so quickly to hate? ______________________

Why was Tamar wearing a richly ornamented robe?

____

Describe the reactions of the following individuals to the crime against Tamar in verses 19-22.

Tamar: ______________________

Absalom: ______________________

David: ______________________

These verses are replete with tragedy. The focus of this corruption was a beautiful young virgin, a daughter of the king. The events of 2 Samuel 13 are scandalous even by today's standards and as painful as the horrid descriptions of rapes we read in a big city paper.

The tragic irony of Tamar's dress touches my heart. The richly ornamented robe was her cloak of dignity and honor. She ripped the fabric of her robe as surely as Amnon had ripped the fabric of her honor. His crime against her was heinous.

Our first reaction is to assign appropriate responsibility. All wrong, fault, and blame for the rape belongs to the perpetrator—Amnon. Strangely, but typically, however, Tamar also fell victim to all three men surrounding this event. Consider Amnon, Absalom, and David's roles in Tamar's life.

Amnon was David's firstborn. Ironically, his name means "trustworthy" and "faithful." Obviously he was neither. Bathsheba and Tamar were described by the same adjective in our first introductions to each of them.

According to 11:2 and 13:1, both women were ______.

Like his father, Amnon saw something beautiful and determined to have it. He gave no consideration to the other party involved. Only his lust mattered. He literally became sin-sick to the point of stopping at nothing to satisfy his appetite. Tamar pled with him to spare her disgrace and his reputation, but "he refused to listen." I found one of the most sickening moments in this tragic event to be Amnon's immediate reaction afterward. We are told Amnon hated Tamar with intense hatred.

Absalom. Absalom discovered his sister in extreme distress. He guessed the nature of the crime against her from the tearing of the virgin's robe. No one can doubt Absalom's love for his sister, but his reaction to her could only have added further injury. Countless victims of rape and molestation have been hurt by similar advice. Absalom told her to "be quiet" and not "take this thing to heart" (v. 20). Absalom's advice to Tamar was to keep the secret and pretend nothing happened.

Unfortunately, Absalom took his own advice. He never said a word to Amnon, either good or bad. But Absalom's hatred for Amnon would finally cause Absalom to lose control. You see, overwhelming feelings cannot be stuffed. They invariably turn inward, take the person prisoner, then often force a break out with tragic consequences.

Absalom was wrong to tell Tamar to be quiet and not take it to heart. The shame was crushing her to pieces. He minimized the significance of the crime against her. She was invited to live with him, but she was not invited to be honest with him. She was left desolate—like the living dead.

David. How did David react (v. 21)? We see just one description—he was furious. What did he do about the crime? Absolutely nothing. Why didn't David take control of his family tragedy? I believe the enemy may have been working on David just as he works on us when we really blow it. Satan uses sin and failure so effectively against us that even after sincere repentance we often remain completely disabled. David allowed his own sense of guilt to handicap him as a parent. Has this ever happened to you?

Bring Home the Banished

Read 2 Samuel 13:23-39. Two years had passed since Amnon's crime against Tamar. List in the margin any evidence that shows Absalom was counting on his father's unwillingness to attend his celebration.

How did the first report David received differ from the truth? ______________________________

Notice Jonadab was the one who told the king not to be concerned because only Amnon was dead. How was Jonadab identified in verse 3? ______________

Do you see any evidence in verse 32 that the "shrewd" Jonadab might have played both sides of the conflict between Amnon and Absalom? Explain in the margin.

What was the condition of David's sons when they returned? ______________________________

Two years passed with bitterness multiplying in Absalom's heart. That's the nature of bitterness. It never stays in its cage. Absalom waited for an opportunity. He devised an elaborate scheme to summon Amnon to his house. The time of sheep shearing was a festive occasion with huge family celebrations. Absalom seized the opportunity, counting on his father to continue in distancing himself from family obligations and celebrations. When David refused to come, Absalom requested Amnon's presence in his place, assuming no one would be suspicious. Customarily, the oldest son represented his father in the father's absence.

David may have been suspicious since he questioned Absalom's choice, but he may have concluded no grounds existed to refuse Amnon the right to attend the celebration. David sent Amnon and the rest of his sons—never to see his eldest again. You may have noticed Absalom did not take the sword to Amnon himself, but, like his father, involved subordinates in the crime. Irony rings from the mouth of a coward who shoves others into action with the words, "Be strong and brave" (v. 28).

Jonadab reared his ugly head in another scandalous scheme. He would never have known Absalom's plans had he not become his confidant. I wonder if he ever told Absalom that he was the one who devised the scheme against Tamar. Not likely. The tragedy ends with one son dead, one son missing, and one father grief stricken. David had two responses toward Absalom after Amnon's death: He mourned for him and longed for him. How odd. Remember when David became furious over Amnon's sin but did nothing? He had the appropriate feelings but inappropriate actions. Once again David felt the right thing and did the wrong thing.

Read 2 Samuel 14:1-33. Why do you think Joab might have devised a method somewhat like a parable to get through to David? ______________________________

What did David decide in verse 24? ________________

Briefly describe Absalom's appearance: ______________

How long did Absalom live in Jerusalem "without seeing the king's face"? ______________________________

Absalom finally got Joab's attention. He set his field on fire. From his method of getting attention, what general statement can you make about Absalom at this point? ____________________________________

Was the meeting between David and Absalom what you expected or did you imagine their reunion differently? Explain in the margin.

Joab obviously had witnessed David's irresponsibility toward Absalom for as long as he intended. He devised a plan to capture David's attention. Through a concocted story of a woman and her prodigal son, Joab convinced David to summon Absalom. I believe Joab used this method because he had seen God use a similar approach through the prophet Nathan once before (2 Sam. 12:1-7)!

David granted Joab's request and allowed him to summon Absalom. Joab was so thrilled that he "fell face to the ground … and he blessed the king" (v. 22). Joab joyfully hastened to bring the young man home, no doubt picturing the emotional but wonderful reunion of this father and son. He brought Absalom back to Jerusalem, bracing himself and his charge for the glorious reunion. He was met with these words from the king: "He must go to his own house; he must not see my face" (v. 24).

The scene had all the right ingredients: Absalom bowing down; the king kissing his son. Only one thing was missing—the heart. The actions of David and his son were generated by custom not emotion. Fearing his son would do something more than set Joab's field on fire, David summoned Absalom to appease him, not accept him. Absalom sought his father's face to force David to look him in the eye, not to beg forgiveness.

Some things in life are do-overs. God sometimes gives us a second chance to do something right. Some chances never come back around. The chance for David and Absalom to be completely reunited in their hearts would not come again. By the time David finally received Absalom, his son's heart was cold.

An Abandoned Throne

Today we will see evidence of Absalom's deep dissatisfaction about his encounter with his father. Their meeting did nothing but fuel his bitterness. The relationship between David and Absalom teaches us an important lesson: Reuniting and reconciliation can be two very different things.

Read 2 Samuel 15:1-12. Where would Absalom stand?

____

Explain in the margin what you think Absalom was trying to accomplish in verse 4.

According to verse 12, Absalom tried not only to steal the hearts of the people but also to steal David's counselor Ahithophel. Why do you think he might have wanted Ahithophel? ____________________________

The revenge Absalom had taken on Amnon's life was not enough. He still cried out for vengeance and was determined his father would pay. Absalom tried everything he knew—good and bad—to get his father's attention. He could not get to David through his home, so he determined to get to him through the throne.

Absalom had specific reasons for every move he made. Each morning he arrived with a chariot and an entourage of men and horses. He looked impressive as he stood at the gate to the city. Absalom called out to anyone entering the city with a complaint, making those individuals feel important.

Absalom worked his scheme for one reason—to steal the hearts of the men of Israel. He continued to work through every step of his plan for four years, waiting for the right moment to attempt an overthrow.

Absalom spent two years waiting for David to punish Amnon, three years in hiding after killing Amnon, two years in Jerusalem waiting for

David to receive him, and four years working his plan against his father. Unforgiveness and retaliation stole eleven years of his life! Eleven years is a long time for anyone to seethe and harbor such bitterness.

Absalom may have been miserable, but he was not dumb. If his plan had been a chess game, stealing Ahithophel was checkmate. Ahithophel was a highly respected advisor and Bathsheba's grandfather, thicker than blood with David. "And so the conspiracy gained strength" (v. 12).

Read 2 Samuel 15:13-37. What did David do when he heard the news of Absalom's conspiracy? ___________

According to verse 30, where did David and all the people go?_______________________________________

In the margin write what David's prayer was concerning Ahithophel.

Is this the same David God anointed as His chosen king? How could he run from his throne? David found himself right in the middle of a cycle of self-appointed failure. Stricken with grief and dressed for mourning, he and his loyal followers trudged the Mount of Olives. There on the Mount of Olives, continuing up to the summit, an amazing thing happened: "David prayed" (v. 31). Little by little, things began to happen. David had run from his throne practically hopeless. "We must flee, or none of us will escape from Absalom" (v. 14). But somewhere on top of that mountain, David got down on his knees and prayed. See his prayer for yourself. God had him write it down. It's Psalm 3. Turn there and read it now. God did not answer every one of David's requests immediately, but He returned enough strength to David for him to begin walking in faith, not fear.

Traitors and Friends

The conflict in the kingdom rekindled old supporters of Saul who were still nursing grudges against David.

Read 2 Samuel 16:1-14. Write in the margin what Ziba was telling David about Mephibosheth.

Why do you think David might have so readily believed he had been betrayed by Mephibosheth?

____

What did David give Ziba? ______________

How did Abishai respond to Shimei's actions toward David? ______________________

Why wouldn't David let Abishai defend him? ________

Restate David's hope in verse 12 in your own words:

____

Have you ever noticed how mean-spirited people will kick a person when he's down? The moment David appeared vulnerable opportunists descended on him like vultures. David had no reason to disbelieve Ziba. If Absalom, his own flesh and blood, could betray him, why not the adult son he adopted? David had suffered so much betrayal that he assumed no one was beyond turning on him.

Nothing makes us as vulnerable as family problems. Personal difficulties may cause us to lack discernment. David told Ziba he would give him everything Mephibosheth owned without confirming Ziba's claims. David's vulnerability caused him to believe the worst and respond with haste rather than prudence. We are wise to be careful about the decisions and assumptions we make when we are stressed. We will tend to react rather than respond.

On the heels of Ziba's claims about Mephibosheth, David encountered a vile man by the name of Shimei. He was profane and violent. He began to curse David and throw stones at the deposed king. The stones hit David, yet I have a feeling the words hurt more than the stones. The man's actions were wrong, but David feared his words might be right.

Through all his ups and downs, victories and failures, we've never seen David walk through this kind of humiliation.

Consider the timing of David's obstacle—just as David was regaining a shred of strength! Coincidental? No way! Just when Satan suspects we are regaining a spark of hope, he hastens to greet us with discouragement and rejection. Notice David's response to Abishai's request to avenge David's persecution: "My son, who is of my own flesh, is trying to take my life. How much more, then, this Benjamite! Leave him alone" (v. 11).

Sometimes when we're down, it's hard to see how many people have come to our aid.

Read 2 Samuel 16:15–17:29. In the margin list the names of everyone who came to David's aid.

We will have missed the turning point of the conflict between David and Absalom if we miss the importance of God "frustrating" Ahithophel's advice. Absalom's decision not to follow his counsel led to David's upper hand in the battle for the kingdom. Ahithophel was a traitor to his king.

Why did Ahithophel betray David while Hushai remained faithful? Hushai risked exposure and death by entering the household of the enemy. He helped buy time for his king by "counseling" and deceiving Absalom so David could strengthen his forces. Why did Hushai respond so differently to a leader who appeared to be on his way out? First Chronicles 27:33 offers a beautiful explanation.

Fill in the blanks from 1 Chronicles 27:33. Ahithophel was the king's _________________. Hushai the Arkite was the king's _________________.

If Only . . .

Read 2 Samuel 18:1-18. Answer the following questions in the margin. (1) Why do you think David might

have wanted to lead the battle himself? (2) Why didn't David's men want him to go to battle? (3) What were David's specific instructions to Joab? (4) Who heard David giving this order to each commander? (5) What strange accident happened to Absalom? (6) How does the soldier represent a direct contrast to Joab in verses 10-14? (7) Why do you think Joab killed Absalom even though he had been commanded to spare him? (8) What did Joab and his men do with Absalom's body? (9) According to verse 18, what had Absalom done during his lifetime?

Like departing words on a tombstone, we read Absalom's eulogy in verse 18: "Absalom had taken a pillar and erected it in the King's Valley as a monument to himself." At first glance, the verse seems to fit the chapter like a square peg in a round hole. At second glance, the passage relates perfectly to the verse before it.

What did the soldiers do after they threw Absalom's body in a big pit in the forest? ____________________

I see great irony in the fact that the record of Absalom's grave and the account of the monument he erected to himself appear together in Scripture. The verses demonstrate that Absalom's death as a traitor remains far more memorable than his self-absorbed life.

Read 2 Samuel 18:19-33. What did David say when he realized Absalom was dead? ____________________

The last words of chapter 18 put chills up a parent's spine, don't they? Suddenly, a heart of tragically suppressed love exploded. Tears David should have cried long ago poured from his eyes. Words he should have said the moment he first saw his prodigal finally burst from his lips: "O my son, Absalom! My son, my son Absalom!" David did not speak about Absalom. He spoke right to him, as if his voice would carry to the depths of the pit where Absalom's body lay. "If only I had died instead of you!" Death would have been far easier for David than life without Absalom.

NOTES

To the Leader:

This lesson zeros in on family conflict. In David's situation, things moved from bad to worse. Such family estrangement might be the case for some of the learners in your group or class setting. As much as possible, emphasize how it is better to deal with family strife initially rather than let it linger and slip out of control, as was the case for David. Be aware that this is a sensitive subject. Estrangement between loved ones is painful. Again, be very sensitive to this.

Before the Session

1. In advance of class, ask your church leadership about resources available for families in crisis. Make this resource information available during the class. Inform learners about the resources that are available for those who need them or for those who know of someone who needs confidential help with a family crisis.
2. A large volume of Scripture is explored in this week's lesson. As you prepare, determine how to best use key passages to emphasized the focus of this lesson.

During the Session

1. Using the interactive activities on page 70, review the events of 2 Samuel 13:1-22. Ask: *When someone wrongs you or wrongs someone close to you, what is your typical reaction? Does your reaction look more like that of David, of Tamar, or of Absalom? Why do you think this is the case?* Explain that David's family was in crisis. Reemphasize David's reaction to the events. Ask: *Why do you suppose David didn't do anything about Amnon's raping of Tamar?* Point out and then discuss the observation made in the last paragraph of Day 1—that David's own sense of guilt could have prevented him from acting as a parent to his children. Ask: *Has this ever happened to you?*
2. Allow learners to summarize the events of 2 Samuel 13:23-39. Explain that this tragic story shows how strife continued to destroy David's family. Ask: *How has conflict affected your family and relatives? Are you connected to most of your relatives? Why or why not?*
3. Allow learners to briefly summarize 2 Samuel 14:1-33. Ask: *Why do you think Absalom and David's reunion was such a complicated situation? Do you think either of the two men were really willing to totally open themselves up to the other?* Emphasize what Day 2's lesson points out: "By the time David finally received Absalom, his son' heart was cold." Ask learners to discuss the dangers of a cold heart.
4. Ask: *What word would you use to describe the reunion of David and Absalom? Why is it hard to use the word* reconciled *when describing*

NOTES

these two men? Allow learners time to review together the succession of events in 2 Samuel 15 as explained in Day 3. Explain that David seemed like a different man. No longer was he courageous and confident. Ask: *Why was David so disarmed? What was the key to David regaining perspective and strength?* If time permits, read Psalm 3 together as a class in order to observe the prayer David uttered as he fled Jerusalem. Ask: *What do you do when things start to cave in around you? What is your first reaction? How does God fit into your crisis resolution plan?*

5. Ask: *How do you determine who is really your friend? How do you determine who is really your adversary?* Allow learners to share the names of those who chose to betray or curse David. Lead learners in identifying who came to David's aid. As a class, read aloud 1 Chronicles 27:33. Ask: *What is the difference between an advisor and a friend? Who would you describe as a good friend, especially when life and circumstances go bad?* Challenge learners to be like Hushai, the friend.
6. Allow learners to reflect on their answers to the set of interactive activities at the beginning of Day 5 on pages 78-80. In particular, allow learners to reflect on why David wasn't wanted on the battlefield. Say: *Absalom was out of control; this pained David.* Then ask: *How do you feel when someone you love is out of control?* Encourage learners to imagine how David must have felt as he paced back and forth awaiting news of Absalom's fate. Ask: *If David had intervened back when Amnon raped Tamar, do you think things would have been different in 2 Samuel 18? Why or why not?* Remind learners that David was still dealing with the legacy of his past sin and its affect on his family. God loved David. Yet the consequences of his sin still abounded.
7. Ask: *When you think about your family and other close relationships, where is the sting of estrangement most prominent?* Encourage members to learn from David and Absalom's story. It is better to act swiftly when crises and conflicts emerge. Otherwise, things quickly can spiral out of control!

Back Where He Belonged

Crossing the Jordan

DIGITAL VIDEO

If you would be interested in hearing Beth Moore discuss the material in this *MasterWork* lesson for April 13—and more—go to *www.lifeway.com* and purchase your personal copy of "Back Where He Belonged," Beth's video for Session 9 of *A Heart Like His.*

Read 2 Samuel 19:1-14. Based on their responses to David's grief, how do you believe David's men felt about him? ___________________________

How would you characterize Joab's method of motivating David to get back to work? ___________

Do you think Joab may have had a personal reason for not wanting to see David mourning? If so, what was the reason? ___________________________

David realized the tribes of Israel were in a quandary because they had alienated their king and pledged allegiance to a leader who was now dead. David responded by appealing to his own tribe, Judah, suggesting they lead the way for Israel in restoring the throne to its rightful king. He would receive his people back without punishing the general population, but he had every intention of making some changes.

What major change is listed in verse 13? ___________

How did the people of Judah accept David's message according to verse 14? ___________________

Joab did not confront King David as a friend. He approached him as commander over the king's armies. He had the best interest of his soldiers in mind and not the emotional well-being of a mourning father. Joab was the same man who thrust the javelins into Absalom's heart. He had seen many lives stolen in battle.

David concluded Joab's advice was right. David returned to the business of the kingdom, but he decided to replace Joab with Amasa. Verse 8 tells us David got up and took his seat in the gateway. The text proceeds with the words, "When the men were told … they all came before him." The words represented a pivotal moment—the king became accessible once more. David was back—in his heart—if not yet on his throne. "He won over the hearts of all the men of Judah as though they were one man" (v. 14).

Now we are about to meet David's first welcoming party.

Read 2 Samuel 19:15-30. According to verse 15, why did the men of Judah come to Gilgal? ____________

Compare 2 Samuel 19:21 to 2 Samuel 16:9. Abishai was obviously itching for a chance to kill Shimei! David responded to Abishai's intentions the same way each time: "What do you and I have in common, you sons of Zeruiah?" (v. 22).

What do you think David meant by this expression?

____

Do you see any evidence in verses 24-30 that suggests Mephibosheth's loyalty to David and his innocence in Ziba's former claims? If so, record it in the margin.

Either David was attempting to end the rivalry as simply as possible or he was testing Mephibosheth's heart when he ordered the land to be split. Mephibosheth's integrity emerged as he responded, in effect, "Let Ziba have everything as long as I have you back safely." Mephibosheth's response was wise and an example of humility and gratefulness.

Read 2 Samuel 19:31-43. Reconsider the tender scene between David and Barzillai. Why did David want Barzillai to stay with him in Jerusalem?____________

Why did Barzillai refuse David's offer? ____________

Based on your impressions of verses 41-43, what was the problem between the men of Israel and the men of Judah? ____________

Second Samuel 19 ends with business as usual. The king crossed the Jordan with an entourage escorting him back to his throne, and before he could dry off his feet, his folks were in a fight.

Returning to a former relationship or position isn't always easy. Going home isn't always fun, especially when infighting awaits you. The smoke David was seeing between Israel and Judah was coming from a fire that had only begun to blaze. Going home was not going to be easy, but across the Jordan River was David's promised land. He had been chosen by God to perform a difficult task. Doing the right thing is rarely the easy thing.

day Two

Unfinished Business

David had ample business to settle as he returned to his post.

Read 2 Samuel 20:1-26. Consider Sheba, son of Bicri. Describe in the margin the kind of man who could incite an army to follow him and desert their king.

Why did Joab kill Amasa? (Review 2 Sam. 19:13 if necessary.) ____________

Why did Amasa's body have to be moved? ____________

How close did Joab's army come to besieging the entire city of Abeh Beth Maacah in order to seize Sheba? ____________

How did the woman who confronted Joab prove herself wise? ____________________________________

David should have known Joab was not going to clean out his desk and resign peaceably. He forced his way back into his former position by killing Amasa, the man David had chosen to replace him.

Another fact makes Joab's actions against Amasa considerably more heinous. According to 1 Chronicles 2:16-17, what was the relationship between Amasa and Joab?____________________________________

Power was so important to Joab he did not stop at spilling his own family's blood. I was a little amused over Joab's words in 2 Samuel 20:2: "Far be it from me to swallow up or destroy!" Joab meant to cause Amasa's death, but he didn't mean to cause a traffic jam. We may have witnessed the first reference to rubber-necking: "Amasa lay wallowing in his blood in the middle of the road, and the man saw that all the troops came to a halt there" (v. 12).

As the plot thickened in the twentieth chapter, one woman was willing to become more than a spectator to imminent disaster, and an entire city was spared. We don't even know her name. She wasn't looking for recognition. She was looking for her city's salvation. An entire village could have perished because one person was such a troublemaker.

Read 2 Samuel 21:1-14. Why did a famine fall on the land for three years? ______________________________

What did God do after recompense was paid to the Gibeonites and David had the bones of Saul and Jonathan moved to the tomb of his father (v. 14)?

____

Many years later the people of Israel were still suffering the ill effects of a king who was rebellious to God. God was holding Israel to an old vow made with the Gibeonites generations prior to David's reign. I think you will find the circumstances of the vow interesting in Joshua 9:1-21.

God meant for His people to be good for their word. He still does. Surely one reason He expects His people to be good for their word is so that observers might come to believe God is good for His. Israel had to keep her agreement with the Gibeonites even though they should never have entered the agreement. Saul broke the agreement with the probable aid of his sons and tried to annihilate a people innocent of their father's sins. Ironically, Saul's sons were brought to account for their father's sins.

The Israelites recommitted themselves to the vow they made with the Gibeonites by satisfying the demands of the Gibeonites. David gave the Gibeonites what they asked and the rain fell and the famine ended.

As rain drenched her hair, a grieving mother gathered her sackcloth and returned home. The mental image of a mother guarding her sons' bodies from predators was obviously more than David could shake. The image reawakened old pictures from years past that disturbed him deeply—the exposed bodies of Saul and his dear friend Jonathan (1 Sam. 31). Their remains were not where they belonged.

David did not send a soldier for their bones. He went for them himself. He gathered them, brought them back, and "they buried the bones of Saul and his son Jonathan in the tomb of Saul's father Kish, at Zela in Benjamin, and did everything the king commanded" (2 Sam. 21:14). Obedience has amazing effects: "After that, God answered prayer in behalf of the land."

An Old Enemy

Read 2 Samuel 21:15-22. Who was the battle between? ______________________

What did Abishai do for David? ______________

Why did David's men insist he not accompany them to battle anymore? ______________________

How many battles with the Philistines are mentioned in verses 15-22? ______________________

The *New International Version* begins verse 15 with, "Once again there was a battle." The next thing we know "David ... became exhausted." I need to know that others have experienced the weariness of fighting the same old enemy over and over. The original word for *exhausted* in Hebrew is *uwph.* It means "to cover, to fly, faint, flee away." It is the overwhelming desire to run and hide.

God led David to victory through all four of the battles mentioned in 2 Samuel 21:15-22, but He brought the victory to David through a few heroes—David's "mighty men" (2 Sam. 23:8-39). God humbled David and made him depend on them for his life. None of us will escape this important life lesson. God will allow us to become exhausted and force us to receive help.

Heroes get tired too. Getting weary is no shame. The shame comes in refusing to accept the victory through another when God supplies a hero. A hero accepts help. Remember, genuine martyrs are never self-appointed.

A Great Celebration

Read 2 Samuel 22:1. On what occasions did David present these words to the Lord? ____________________

Sometimes God puts a new song in our mouths—a hymn of praise to our God! Other times, He brings us back to an old song.

The first verse of 2 Samuel 22 tells us David remembered the words he had sung many years before after God delivered him from the hand of Saul. Why had his recent victory over the Philistines rekindled the remembrance of his victory over Saul? I believe there might have been several similarities: 1. Both conflicts seemed they would never end. 2. Both conflicts sapped his strength. 3. Both conflicts caused him to rely on another's strength.

Decades wedged their way between the solos of this one song.

Read 2 Samuel 22:1-51 and respond in the margin to the following items: (1) List every name, object, or role by which David referred to God. (2) Which verses and phrases describe God in such a way that you are awed by Him? (3) Which verses and phrases describe how God readies His warrior(s) for battle? (4) Which verses and phrases testify that God blesses the obedient? (5) Which verses and phrases acknowledge God's Word? (6) Which verses and phrases remind you that God hears the cries of His children? (7) To which one verse can you most readily relate? Why?

The Book of 2 Samuel is not the only place David's words of victory are found. Turn to Psalm 18. You'll find an almost identical set of verses to those in 2 Samuel 22. One of the exceptions is too precious to miss.

Write Psalm 18:1.______________________________

"I love you, Lord." No demands. No despair. Just I love you. The words might seem more fitting as the grand finale rather than the opening line. Their sudden appearance suggests they were words that could not wait. The psalmist considered his delivered estate and his Father's stubborn love, and he burst forth with the words: "I love you, Lord."

If 2 Samuel 22 and Psalm 18 compel us to see one thing, it is that God is a personal God we each can call our own. He is my Strength when I am weak. He is my Rock when I am slipping. He is my Deliverer when I am trapped. He is my Fortress when I am crumbling. He is my Refuge when I am pursued. He is my Shield when I am exposed. He is my Lord when life spins out of control.

A Hand Withdrawn

Read 2 Samuel 24:1-17. In verse 1, God's anger was directed to ____________________________.

What options did God give David? ____________________

What happened when the angel stretched out his hand to destroy Jerusalem? ____________________________

At what exact location did the angel stop the plague?

____

The first verse of chapter 24 says, "He [God] incited David against them, saying, 'Go and take a census of Israel and Judah.' " A brief look at this verse may cause us to wonder why God would ask David to do something and then kill 70,000 people as a result.

Sometimes we can understand passages or events by comparing these "parallel" accounts.

First Chronicles 21:1 sheds a little light on what happened to David. What does this verse add to what you learned in 2 Samuel 24:1? ____________________________

Who enticed David to sin—God or Satan? ____________________

We can be assured that God did not tempt David to sin and then judge him harshly for it. God did, however, allow David to be tempted because He saw something in David's heart that needed to be exposed.

Now consider a second matter. Did the punishment exceed the crime? If we are not careful to study the text, 70,000 men seemed to die solely as a result of David's sin. Although David's actions no doubt displeased God and caused judgment, 2 Samuel 24:1 clearly states the Lord's anger burned against *Israel.* We do not know why God's anger burned against Israel.

Some suggest God may have been judging Israel for their quickness to desert David, God's sovereign choice, and follow Absalom. In Scripture you will almost never see God's hand move in a major act of judgment except over blatant and continued rebellion with an unwillingness to repent.

Why was David also wrong? I'd like to suggest three possible reasons.

1. He deserted the throne God had given him and did not trust God to fight his battles for him. Earlier David trusted God to direct his battles and to fight them for him. This time David ignored God and depended on human resources and wisdom.

2. He did not stand in the gap and intercede for the sins of his nation as Moses did. God revoked a portion of His judgment on Israel as a direct result of the humility and intercession of Moses. David saw the evil ways of his nation and did not intercede nor take any responsibility.

3. He possessed wrong motives for taking the census. David fell to the temptation of counting his fighting men out of the sins of pride or distrust or both. Anyway, as king of Israel, David's heart was wrong toward God. God had proved Himself many times in the life of this king. David had no grounds for pride or distrust.

Based on 2 Samuel 24 and 1 Chronicles 21, David and the people of Israel shared the responsibility for the judgment handed down to them. Yet in the heart of this difficult account of anger and judgment is God's mercy. Reread 2 Samuel 24:15-16. *Exactly when* did God grieve? When the angel stretched out his hand to destroy Jerusalem. *Exactly where* was the angel of the Lord at the time? The threshing floor of Araunah the Jebusite. Read further so you may revel in the special significance of this threshing floor and the mercy God poured out at this place.

Read 2 Samuel 24:18-25. What did Gad tell David to do on the threshing floor? ______________________

What reason did David give Araunah for building the altar? ______________________

When Araunah offered to give it to David, how did David respond? ______________________

According to 1 Chronicles 21:27–22:1, what else was to happen on this exact location?________________

According to 2 Chronicles 3:1, the temple, thus the threshing floor, was located on Mount ____________.

The exact location of the threshing floor of Araunah the Jebusite was the most vital place in Israel's history. Scripture says God grieved when the angel reached the threshing floor of Araunah the Jebusite and stretched out his hand to destroy Jerusalem. The original Hebrew word for *grieve* in this passage is *nacham,* meaning "to draw breath forcibly, pant, breathe strongly; to groan; to be sorry; to pity; to grieve; to have compassion, to comfort oneself." *Nacham* carries the idea of breathing deeply as "a physical display of one's feeling, usually sorrow, compassion, or comfort." The word was used once before in 2 Samuel 12:24 in which it means "being consoled over the death of an infant child."[1]

When the angel of the Lord stretched out his hand at the threshing floor of Araunah the Jebusite, God seemed to cry. He "panted" in grief somewhat like one "being consoled over the death of an infant child." I want to suggest that the primary reason God grieved as if over the death of a child at that exact location was related to an event that took place on that very soil many years before.

Read Genesis 22:1-2, then skim the remainder of the chapter. What general event does this pivotal chapter record? ________________________________

Where did this event take place according to Genesis 22:2? ________________________________

God did not coincidentally grieve at this exact spot generations later during David's reign, then coincidentally direct an altar, and ultimately the temple of God, to be built there as well. Each occurrence was based on the vivid lesson God taught about substitutionary death at the same location. Look at the similarities!

The altar. God commanded that an altar for sacrifice be built by both Abraham and David—and ultimately by Solomon—on the same spot.

The timing. Genesis 22:10-12 tells us that when Abraham reached out his hand and took the knife to slay his son, God intervened and stopped him. God then presented a sacrifice in his place. Consider the timing during David's reign. First Chronicles 21:16 tells us, "David looked up and saw the angel of the Lord standing between heaven and earth, with a drawn sword in his hand extended over Jerusalem." Of the same event, 2 Samuel 24:16 says, "When the angel stretched out his hand to destroy Jerusalem, the Lord was grieved because of the calamity and said to the angel who was afflicting the people, 'Enough: Withdraw your hand.' The angel of the Lord was then at the threshing floor of Araunah the Jebusite." In both cases, the moment God saw a sword raised to destroy life at this location, He intervened and accepted substitutionary sacrifices. That both of these events happened at the same place and at the moment a sword was being drawn is no accident.

The day Abraham offered Isaac pictured the cross as the ultimate altar of sacrifice and the substitutionary death of the unblemished Lamb as the perfect sacrifice. Many years later, during David's reign, God saw the angel raise his sword over the lives of His people at that same location and He grieved and said "Enough!" *Why?* Because when God saw the threshing floor at Mount Moriah, He saw *mercy,* mercy that would finally be complete on Calvary when God would look on the suffering of His Son and be satisfied (Isa. 53:11).

We must meditate for a moment on David's words as Araunah offered him the threshing floor free of charge. David said, "I will not sacrifice to the Lord my God burnt offering that cost me nothing." Mount Moriah did not represent a cheap offering. The sacrifice depicted on that mountain throughout the ages was costly. Abraham's sacrifice cost him dearly. God's sacrifice cost Him severely. The chastened king's sacrifice was costly as well. At the threshing floor of Araunah, the cost of sacrifice was counted—and God grieved.

---

[1] *The Complete Word Study Dictionary: Old Testament* (Chattanooga, TN: AMG Publishers, 1994), 2339-2340.

Before the Session

1. Bring markers for either a marker board or larger sheets of paper (see # 1 below).
2. Bring 3-by-5-inch note cards for the final lesson application exercise (see # 7 below).
3. A large volume of Scripture is explored in this week's lesson. As you prepare, determine how to best use key passages to emphasized the focus of this lesson.

During the Session

1. The journey described in 2 Samuel 19 was a physical journey across the Jordan River. Yet more importantly it was a journey of David reconnecting relationally with many groups of people. Utilize a marker board or a large sheet of paper to list names of the people (or groups of people) whom David had to relate to while traveling back to the throne. Next to each group, describe how David had to respond in each situation [For example: "Barzillai [bahr-ZIL-igh]—he expressed gratitude"] For additional help in constructing the list, utilize the interactive activities found in Day 1.
2. As a class, briefly summarize the events of 2 Samuel 20. Utilize the interactive activities for Day 2 to expedite the discussion. Ask: *After studying all the stories about Joab, what is apparent about his character? In your context, how do you handle people like Joab who behave ambitiously?*
3. Briefly review 2 Samuel 21. Once again utilize the interactive activities for Day 2 to expedite the review of 2 Samuel 21. Ask: *Why was it so important for Saul's blood-guilt to be dealt with so many years after his death? What does this story teach us about the troubling impact of sin?*
4. Briefly summarize the Focal Passage of 2 Samuel 21:15-22 for Day 3. Use the Day 3 interactive activities to facilitate discussion. Ask: *Why do you think David had to struggle to defend himself in battle?* Explain that David had aged and his agility on the battlefield

NOTES

To the Leader:

David aged and his reign was coming to an end. In the same way, as we age, our role in life changes. Learners are all experiencing change, whether in their twenties or their eighties. As you discuss the life of David, be aware that this lesson helps us understand how to age and grow old gracefully. We can learn to appreciate the experiences of life and also learn to pass along traditions. At the same time, use this lesson to show how David's age didn't affect his usefulness. God continued to use David to the very end of his life. God is not limited by our age or by our stamina.

NOTES

had waned. Heroes stepped in to defend and represent Israel. Ask: *How do you feel when it seems someone else can do a better job at something you once excelled at?* Allow time for older learners to deal with their emotional responses to aging.

5. Ask: *If you could pick one verse in 2 Samuel 22 to describe how God relates to you, which would it be? Why?* Refer to the interactive activity on the top of page 88 to facilitate the discussion of the above question, or allow learners time to complete the activity. Encourage learners to give examples as to why they chose their particular verse. Read aloud Psalm 18:1. Ask: *Starting from the beginning of his life until this moment in Scripture, what specific events do think helped David come to his conclusion found in Psalm 18:1?*
6. Ask: *Based on 2 Samuel 24:1-17 and 1 Chronicles 21:1, what caused God's anger to fall on Israel?* Explain that this story is hard to understand but that the underlying theme is that sin was affecting God's relationship with both David and with Israel. Ask: *What was significant about the threshing floor of Araunah* [uh-ROO-nuh]*? What would eventually be established on this site?* Direct learners to reflect on the interactive activities of Day 5 on the top of page 91 that focus on 1 Chronicle 21:27–22:1 and on 2 Chronicles 3:1. Ask: *What is the significance and connection of the threshing floor with Genesis 22:1-2?* Using the Day 5 material, spend time reviewing the significance of God's activity at the threshing floor location. Ask: *How do the events found in Genesis and 2 Samuel foreshadow the act of sacrifice Christ would offer hundreds of years later?*
7. To conclude this lesson, allow learners time to review how David's life changed as he aged. Challenge learners to consider how they can change gracefully as they age and grow old. Challenge learners to take a 3 by 5 inch note card and complete the following sentence: "One way God can use me right now is: ______________________." Instruct learners to keep this card close to them as they go through their daily routines this week. Affirm that, like David, we are always useful to God, no matter what stage of life we are in.

The Final Years and Settled Fears

A Breath of Life

Read 1 Kings 1:1-27. At what point in David's life does this book open, and what appears to be the state of his health? ______________________________

What impact on Adonijah's life do you think David's lack of discipline might have had? ______________

Identify whether each person was for (F) Adonijah or against (A) him. ___ Joab ____ Nathan the prophet ____ Abiathar the priest ____ Zadok the priest

Nathan was the prophet God used to confront the sin between David and Bathsheba. He was also the one who warned Bathsheba about Adonijah's plans, which probably would have resulted in death for her and Solomon. Nathan showed himself to be a true prophet of God. He could both confront sin and lovingly care for sinners.

I am saddened by the initial words of 1 Kings: "When King David was old and well advanced in years." The words suggest the inevitable to us. Perhaps more difficult to consider are the words that followed: "He could not keep warm even when they put covers over him." I am almost shocked by his sudden mortality. As he lay chilled beneath the weight of heavy blankets, we realize his humanity and his frailty. By the standards of his day, David was not an extremely old man.

DIGITAL VIDEO

If you would be interested in hearing Beth Moore discuss the material in this *MasterWork* lesson for April 20—and more—go to *www.lifeway.com* and purchase your personal copy of "The Final Years and Settled Fears," Beth's video for Session 10 of *A Heart Like His.*

David's fourth son took quick advantage of his father's failing health and followed in the footsteps of his deceased half brother Absalom. Adonijah did not count on Bathsheba to warn David about his plan.

After a long absence from Scripture, the prophet Nathan reenters the scene. I am touched by his support of David and the union with Bathsheba after acknowledgment of their grave sin. Nathan knew Bathsheba was the key to restoring decision-making strength to the king. Need has a way of breathing fresh life into a soul, if just for a moment. We will see David, who seemed chilled with the onset of death, assume swift control, perform the will of God, and meet the desires of his queen's heart. Whether on his sickbed or on his throne, David was indeed still king.

A New King

Apparently Bathsheba stepped out of the room so Nathan could have full access to the king. Our Scripture reading begins today with David summoning Bathsheba back into his private quarters.

Read 1 Kings 1:28-53. What did David promise Bathsheba? ________________________________

David easily could have issued the orders without Bathsheba being present, but he summoned his queen so he could make an oath to her. The words were addressed directly to Bathsheba, intimating to us that this was a matter not only between king and queen but between husband and wife—father and mother.

David called Zadok, Nathan, and Benaiah (see 2 Sam. 20:23; 23:20) to escort Solomon to his rightful place of authority. Write in the margin what their positions were.

Write in the margin the four commands David gave to Zadok, Nathan, and Benaiah.

David chose a prophet, priest, and warrior to confirm the new king. For the nation to be strong, all four areas of authority needed to be present.

How did the people react to the sound of the trumpet announcing the anointing of Solomon? ______________

Describe David's response to the news of Solomon's anointing. ______________

Why do you think Adonijah took hold of the horns of the altar of sacrifice when he realized Solomon had been anointed king of Israel? ______________

We have seen many pivotal points in David's life. Now we come to one of the most significant turning points. He was passing the kingdom. I can't help but wonder what emotions filled Bathsheba. The crown would be taken from her husband and placed on the head of her son. Did she feel sadness and joy? mourning and celebration? Bathsheba wanted nothing more than for Solomon to receive the crown, but was she prepared for David to have to lose it for Solomon to gain it? Being wife and mother can sometimes feel like two exclusive roles tearing one woman in half. No doubt Bathsheba experienced those feelings. Her husband assured her that Solomon would be king. He was true to his word.

David issued very specific commands regarding Solomon's rise to power. He sent the primary prophet and priest of God to anoint Solomon. In addition, he sent his most trustworthy warrior and his army to protect Solomon. They were to put Solomon on King David's mule and escort him. Customarily, a king rode on a mule to signify his intent to be a servant to the people. The mule was often dressed with a wreath of flowers around its neck or a royal drape over its back.

David specifically commanded the men to escort Solomon to Gihon. Two springs provided Jerusalem's water supply: the En Rogel spring and the Gihon spring.

Look back at 1 Kings 1:9. What was happening at the En Rogel spring? ______________

The Gihon spring was directly east of the city wall. The ancient Hebrew people believed God's glory and authority would come from the east. The Gihon spring did not provide a steady flow but "gushes out at irregular intervals, twice a day in the dry season to four or five times in the rainy season. Water issues from a crack sixteen feet long in the rock." Even the name was significant. The name *Gihon* comes from a Hebrew word which means "a bursting forth."[1] A new king was bursting on the scene to supply the nation of Israel with security and authority.

Zadok the priest took the horn of oil from the sacred tent and anointed Solomon. Could this have been the same horn tipped by the hand of Samuel over the head of a young shepherd boy?

Solomon may not have been the natural choice in the eyes of men. He was not the oldest of the sons of David. Solomon represented God's divine mercy. He was the embodiment of second chances. He was the innocence that came from guilt. He was God's choice.

When David received the news from his royal officials "the king bowed in worship on his bed and said, 'Praise be to the Lord' " (vv. 47-48). This verse records the last time God used the word *king* in the Book of 1 Kings in reference to His beloved David. God chose to pen this last reference to *King* David in a sentence eternally linked to two responses:

- *Worship.* Too weak to move to the floor, David fell on his face right where he was.
- *Praise.* "Praise be to the Lord, the God of Israel, who has allowed my eyes to see a successor on my throne today" (v. 48).

On that last day as king, David bowed to worship. David's actions were often contradictory, but one consistency he wove throughout his life and reign—he was a man of worship, a man after God's own heart.

Wholehearted Devotion

Historians generally agree that David lived somewhere between one and two years after Solomon assumed his reign. God allowed David the strength to prepare the new king for public coronation.

The first order of business for the new king was the building of a house for the name of the Lord. Before he died, the old king gathered the materials and drafted the plans for the work. The Book of 1 Chronicles records the vivid account of the extensive preparations David made before his death (1 Chron. 22:5).

Read 1 Chronicles 22. To what location was David referring in verse 1 when he said, "The house of the Lord God is to be here"? Review 1 Chronicles 21:22-30. ______________________

According to 1 Chronicles 22:5, why did David make preparations for the house to be built for the Lord?

____

How would you characterize Solomon's reign based on the prophecy God gave David in verses 9 and 10?

____

What order did David issue in verse 17? ______________

To what did David tell Solomon and the leaders of Israel to devote their hearts and souls? ______________

In 1 Chronicles 22:14-16 David shared with Solomon all that had been gathered for the building of the sanctuary and all who had been commissioned to help. I find his words so pertinent and applicable to us today: "Now begin the work, and the Lord be with you" (v. 16). In other words, "I've set aside everything you will need. You have all the materials and all the support your task will require. Now get started."

Some of the most important words ever formed on David's tongue are found in 1 Chronicles 22:19: "Now devote your heart and soul to seeking the Lord your God." The original Hebrew word for *devote* is *nathan.* It means "to give, place, add, send forth. *Nathan* indicates … fastening something in place."[2] I especially love the idea this wonderful definition expresses in the word *fastening.* David told Solomon and the leaders of Israel to fasten their hearts to seeking the Lord.

To what is your heart fastened? ____________________

The aged David had also learned a few things about priorities. He knew what he was talking about when he told the leaders of Israel to devote their hearts and souls to seeking the Lord. I don't believe David was looking out for the nation of Israel alone. He was also looking out for his son. One of my most heartfelt pleas before the throne of grace is, *Please surround my children with positive influences. Raise up godly friends for my children!* David knew that little would influence Solomon's success more than being surrounded by leaders whose hearts were devoted to seeking the Lord.

First Chronicles 23–27 documents the organization of Solomon's kingdom under the commands of David. These five chapters bridge David's two proclamations and chronicle the appointment of the Levites and priests to serve God in the temple, the singers to lead His praises, and the army to protect the people.

First Chronicles 23:5 tells us David appointed 4,000 people to praise the Lord with musical instruments. Can you imagine an orchestra of 4,000?

Read 1 Chronicles 28. According to verse 6, who chose Solomon as king?____________________________

What specific commands did David issue Solomon in verse 9? ______________________________

David gave Solomon the plans for the temple, but who had given the plans to David (v. 12)?________________

In verse 9 David gave his son three vital directives we would be wise to obey:

1. Acknowledge God. Acknowledging God first thing every morning transforms my day. Do you daily acknowledge the Lord as Lord of your life?

2. Serve God with wholehearted devotion. The original Hebrew word for *wholehearted* is *shalem* and means "unhewn, untouched stones." In the Old Testament *shalem* often refers to rocks that were uncut. Notice something quite interesting about the temple God commanded Solomon to build. First Kings 6:7 tells us, "In building the temple, only blocks dressed at the quarry were used, and no hammer, chisel or any other iron tool was heard at the temple site while it was being built." Do you see the significance? No stone could be cut in the temple. The uncut stones represented the kind of devotion God was demanding from His nation—*shalem,* wholehearted devotion, uncut hearts. David was used of God to describe *shalem* perfectly in Psalm 86:11: "Teach me your way, O Lord, and I will walk in your truth; give me an undivided heart, that I may fear your name." A divided heart places our entire lives in jeopardy. God uses an undivided heart to keep us out of trouble. David learned the price of a divided heart the hard way. He lived with the repercussions for the rest of his life. Let's just take David's word for it and surrender now! Never forget, God's commands are for our good.

3. Serve God with a willing spirit. The original Hebrew word for *willing* in this reference is *chaphets,* which means "to find pleasure in, take delight in, be pleased with, have an affection for; to desire; to choose; to bend, bow. The main meaning is to feel a strong positive attraction for something, to like someone or something very much."[3] Do you see what God is saying? He wants us to serve Him and honor Him because we want to! Because it pleases us! Because we *choose* to! You see, the Lord searches every heart and understands every motive behind the thoughts!

We will never be men and women after God's own heart with half-hearted devotion. A heart wholly devoted to God is a heart like His.

Praises of the Great Assembly

Today we see the conclusion of David's address to the assembly. We can only imagine the emotions that flooded David's heart. In 1 Chronicles 29:1 David reminded the people: "My son Solomon, the one whom God has chosen, is young and inexperienced." David was looking at a young man bursting with energy, full of plans, rehearsing promises—a young man childishly confident he would never do certain things and would always do others. Solomon lacked nothing but age and experience—a lack that probably scared his father half to death. So David looked at the whole assembly and basically said, "Give him a hand. He's going to need it."

Read 1 Chronicles 29:1-9. What do you think motivated the leaders to give so freely?__________________

According to verse 9, why did the people rejoice?

____

Never underestimate the power of a positive example! David could not motivate the leaders of Israel to give freely and wholeheartedly to the Lord unless he gave. The third verse clearly tells us, "I now give my personal treasures of gold and silver for the temple of my God, over and above everything I have provided for this holy temple."

David gave what was his. The people overwhelmingly responded. Do you give that which is personal? Does your monetary giving come from your heart, not just your checkbook? God delights in the giving of your personal treasures—and others are motivated by your example! I love the way the ninth verse captures the electricity of the moment: "The people rejoiced at the willing response of their leaders, for they had given freely and wholeheartedly to the Lord. David the king also rejoiced greatly." What a glorious moment! I can't think of much that spurs the hearts of the people of God like the wholehearted devotion of their leaders. When leadership is sold out to God, the followers become willing to sell out to Him.

Read 1 Chronicles 29:10-20. What was David saying in verses 10-13? ______________________________

In verse 17 David acknowledged the importance of integrity to God. What does the word *integrity* mean to you? ________________________________

What two things did David request from God in verse 18? ____________________ ____________________

In 1 Chronicles 28:9 David told Solomon to serve God with wholehearted devotion. In 1 Chronicles 29:19 David asked God to give Solomon wholehearted devotion. The wholehearted devotion of a person toward God is obviously a joint work between God and the individual.

When David said, "Praise the Lord your God," what did the people do (v. 20)? ____________________

Praise is an exercise in perspective. Praise reminds us who God is. But praise also reminds us who we are. Notice David's words in verse 14, "But who am I?" Authentic praise works every time! Things seem to fall right in perspective. I don't believe you can truly praise and worship God without ending up with an humbled heart.

Passionate hearts and genuine praises are invariably contagious. David's overflow caused a tidal wave of praise. In verse 20, when David called the whole assembly to praise the Lord their God, "They bowed low and fell prostrate before the Lord and the king." David and his people were overwhelmed with the privilege of giving: "But who am I, and who are my people, that we should be able to give as generously as this?" (v. 14). The enormity of what they had been able to give represented the enormity of what they had been given. And they fell on their faces.

A Resting Place

Read 1 Chronicles 29:21-25. How would you describe the mood of the people the day following David's public address? ____________________

How did the people of Israel respond to their new king? ____________________

Based on verse 25, how did Solomon's kingdom compare to David's? ______________________________

David had no reason to resist death's call. He had turned over his crown and joyfully dedicated his personal riches to the building of the temple. He was too old to conquer kingdoms, too sick to fill a sling, too frail to feast on the fatted calf. But that which he treasured most was never so dear to him and never so real. Scholars generally agree that David wrote the words of Psalm 71 in his old age as he confronted his hastening death.

Read Psalm 71:14. What would David always have that no one could take from him? ______________________

Read Psalm 71:20 carefully. What hope did David have as the cords of death encompassed him? __________

David had hope of the resurrection, just as we do! Not just an empty wish but an anxious and certain expectation!

"Then David rested with his fathers and was buried in the City of David" (1 Kings 2:10).

What is the most significant way God has spoken to you through *A Heart Like His*? ____________________

____

____

[1]Trent C. Butler, ed., *Holman Bible Dictionary* (Nashville: Holman Bible Publishers, 1991), 553.

[2]*The Complete Word Study Dictionary: Old Testament* (Chattanooga, TN: AMG Publishers, 1994), 2344.

[3]*The Complete Word Study Dictionary: Old Testament*, 2317.

NOTES

Before the Session

1. Bring paper and pencils for activity # 7 below.
2. A large volume of Scripture is explored in this week's lesson. As you prepare, determine how to best use key passages to emphasized the focus of this lesson.

During the Session

1. Ask: *Based on 1 Kings 1:1-4, what was happening to David? Based on 1 Kings 1:5-27, what was happening to the kingdom of Israel as David aged?* Emphasize how different people in the story either sided with David or with Adonijah [ad-oh-NIGH-juh]. Ask: *Why would someone logically have sided with Adonijah? Why would it make sense to side with David?* Explain that sometimes trusting God means making decisions that may not seem logical. Ask: *Have you ever had to take sides, choosing to align yourself with one person over another? What happened?*
2. Ask: *How did David solve the dilemma posed by Adonijah's claim on the kingdom?* Review with learners the process David employed to inaugurate Solomon as the king. Utilize the interactive activities of Day 2 to emphasize the thoroughness of David's plan to set up Solomon as king. Ask: *What does David's act of worship at the end of this story tell us about his attitude and character?* Explain that David involved God in the process of passing along the kingdom. This wasn't a mere tactical move on David's part to get his desired successor on the throne. Instead, David sought God's guidance and wisdom. Ask: *How do you involve God in the process of critical decisions you face?*
3. Review the interactive activities on page 99 in Day 3. Ask: Bas*ed on 2 Chronicles 22, how was David training and preparing his son to rule after his death?* Ask learners to share how they responded to the interactive exercise in Day 3 that asked, "To what is your heart fastened?" Emphasize to learners that David understood the priority of God in all things! Review the "three vital directives" offered on pages 100-101. Ask: *What would it look like for us to employ these directives*

To the Leader:

David's life comes to a close in this lesson. David finished well. He also made strategic, God-inspired plans for the future of Israel. Learners need to embrace the fact that they, like David, have an opportunity to leave a legacy in this world. Help learners move from simply living for themselves to a sense of how they can begin living for a greater cause that will outlast their own lives. Help learners recognize that serving God allows them to be part of something infinitely huge! David lived for God's cause, and we can too.

NOTES

in our lives today? In what practical ways can these directives help us at home, at work, and at play? Which of the directives is easiest for you to follow? Which is hardest?

4. Briefly review the details of 1 Chronicles 29:1-9. Ask learners to share how they responded to the interactive activities on the top of page 102. Ask: *What motivates us today to give freely? What hinders us from giving freely?*
5. Ask someone to read aloud 1 Chronicles 29:10-13. Ask: *What events do you think David had in mind when he offered this prayer? Does this prayer reflect the way you typically feel about God? Why or why not?* Read 1 Chronicles 29:19. David asked God to give his son a sense of wholehearted devotion for the Lord and His Word. Ask: *What would it look like for us to live with a sense of wholehearted devotion to the Lord in the world today?*
6. Read 1 Chronicles 29:21-25. Ask: *How was Solomon's reign affected by David's own prior rule as king?* Explain that David sought to finish well. His life was devoted to God, and thus David lived for the cause of Israel's greater good. His efforts to lead with integrity led to the powerful reign of his son Solomon. Indeed, Solomon enjoyed God's blessings, no doubt because of David's rule. Ask: *Do you act as if you want the next generation to experience better days than you experience now? How are you leaving a positive impact for future generations?*
7. Remind learners that David wrote Psalm 71 to celebrate God's faithfulness and watchful care over him all the days of his life. If time permits, distribute paper and pencils and ask learners to compose their own short poem, praising God for leading, guiding, and protecting them throughout the vicissitudes of their lives to this point and stating their commitments to continue to depend on the Lord for the days and years ahead.
8. Celebrate with learners the fact that you have completed this eight-week series. Ask learners to share one way this study of David's life has changed them. Ask learners to share one way they will seek to change their lives in order to live with a greater sense of wholehearted devotion to the Lord.

ABOUT THE WRITERS

Larry Crabb

is a well-known psychologist, speaker, Bible teacher, author, and founder/director of NewWay Ministries. He is scholar in residence at Colorado Christian University and serves as spiritual director of the American Association of Christian Counselors. His many popular books include *Inside Out*, *Finding God*, *Connecting*, *The Safest Place on Earth*, and *SoulTalk*.

AMY SUMMERS wrote the personal learning activities and teaching plans for these lessons. Amy is an experienced writer for LifeWay Bible study curriculum, a wife, a mother, and a Sunday School leader from Arden, North Carolina. She is a graduate of Baylor University and Southwestern Baptist Theological Seminary.

ABOUT THIS STUDY

2-9-09

"As the deer pants for streams of water, so my soul pants for you, O God. My soul thirsts for God, for the living God. When can I go and meet with God? ... Why are you downcast, O my soul? Why so disturbed within me? Put your hope in God, for I will yet praise him, my Savior and my God" (Ps. 42:1-2,11, NIV).

For what was the psalmist yearning? ______________

hope, comfort, peace of mind.

Talk honestly with God about the yearnings and hopes of your heart. Serenity!

The PAPA Prayer

1. Ever ask for something from God that you didn't receive?
2. Ever pray for guidance, especially in a difficult relationship, that never came?
3. Ever really need to hear God's voice and then try to believe you did, even though you weren't sure?
4. Do you sometimes feel that God is turning a deaf ear to your most desperate prayer requests?
5. Have you ever prayed for comfort yet ended up feeling more empty and alone after you prayed?
6. Has praying for strength to overcome temptation ever left you feeling just as weak and the temptation just as strong or even stronger?
7. Do you know God well enough to enjoy His company the same way you enjoy being with a family member or close friend?
8. Do you want to know God better and enjoy Him more than you know and enjoy anyone else?
9. Do you connect with God in such a way that enables you to hear His voice and to know He's right there with you?

Perhaps the frantic pace of life, coupled with a heavy sense of deadness beneath everything you do has left you knowing you were built for more. You're hungry. You long to connect with God so closely that you hear His voice as clearly as a child lost in the woods hears her daddy call her name.

If you can sense these yearnings stirring in your heart, then this study is written to you. It's all about a way to pray, a way to talk to God a little and listen to God a lot, a way to get better acquainted with God—and yourself—through a special kind of two-way conversation, a way to pray that lets you experience His life in you and releases that life to trickle, sometimes gush, out of you into others.

I call it the PAPA prayer.

Larry Crabb

Introducing the Papa Prayer

day One

Knowing God

Ever since I've been a Christian, I've asked God for lots of things He hasn't given. There have been times I've begged God for clear guidance on how to handle messy relationships or in what direction to move in a confusing situation, and it never came. I could name a dozen nasty spots in my life, probably more, when I've felt desperate to hear from God yet heard only silence.

Sometimes I tried to believe I had heard God's voice, but I knew I really hadn't. I wanted it so badly I pretended I had.

"God, where are You?" I've often asked. "Are You listening to me? Do You know what's going on in my life? Do You care? Do I even know who You are?"

"I cry out to you, O God, but you do not answer; I stand up, but you merely look at me" (Job 30:20).

"The LORD has heard my cry for mercy; the LORD accepts my prayer" (Ps. 6:9).

"To you I call, O LORD my Rock; do not turn a deaf ear to me. For if you remain silent, I will be like those who have gone down to the pit" (Ps. 28:1).

Read the Scriptures printed in the margin. Check the verse that best reflects how you're feeling about prayer right now.

In my 52 years as a Christian, I haven't yet known God in the same way I've known people I could see and touch and audibly hear. I know my wife in ways I don't know the Father, and I mean personal ways, not physical ones. I know my sons in ways I don't know God's Son. And I know special friends in ways I don't know God's Spirit.

Read Ezekiel 36:27 in your Bible. We should be able to know God in an even deeper way than we know people because God put His Spirit **in us.**

But all that's changing. Not completely, of course. Complete change comes when we get home. But enough change is going on to give me fresh hope that more is ahead in this life. Something good is happening inside me that's new. Perhaps what encourages me most is that this new hope grows stronger on bad days, and I still have plenty of those.

Knowing my real Papa is meaning more to me. There are moments of encounter with God that are more real and reach deeper and produce more joy than my best encounters with others, including my wife, my kids, and my closest friends.

Emptiness, loneliness, thirst, and hunger still plague me, along with irritability, discouragement, and boredom. I still have dark days. But now these experiences sometimes seem more like open doorways into a better world than thick walls trapping me in this one.

Now when I ask God for things I want, I'm more aware that He's listening. And I feel less demanding, less as if I'm trying to control God, to get Him to do certain things that, right or wrong, matter to me. He wants me to be as happy as He can make me. And I'm realizing for that to happen, I must give up on the happiness I can find elsewhere. That doesn't mean I'm not to enjoy a good meal or good friendship; it means I'm not to depend on or require the good things of life for my well-being, or to figure out how I can get God to give me the legitimate blessings of life that I want—or when I get them, to ask them to fill me up more than they can.

All these changes are directly the work of God. But He's working through a vehicle He's given me. That vehicle is a new understanding of prayer that, although still shallow and perhaps new only to me, is far deeper and richer—and simpler—than anything I've known before.

Would you like to experience this kind of prayer life?

☑ Absolutely **❑ I'm not sure** **❑ No**

If yes, make Jesus' disciples' request in Luke 11:1 your prayer today: "One day Jesus was praying in a certain place. When he finished, one of his disciples said to him, 'Lord, teach us to pray.'"

A New Way of Praying

I've practiced centering prayer. I've contemplatively prayed. I've prayed liturgically. I've interceded and petitioned. The first model of prayer I learned as a kid was ACTS: adoration, confession, thanksgiving, supplication. I tried that too for years. I've benefited from each, and I still do. There are many good ways to pray.

But I believe I've sovereignly stumbled on a fresh way to think about prayer that has led me to a new way of praying. It's not a formula or technique. There are no techniques in good conversation with God. There are no means to manipulate Him, no ways to persuade Him to do things our way. He's not open to input on how best to run my life.

"Here's what I want you to do: Find a quiet, secluded place so you won't be tempted to role-play before God. Just be there as simply and honestly as you can manage. The focus will shift from you to God, and you will begin to sense his grace. The world is full of so-called prayer warriors who are prayer-ignorant. They're full of formulas and programs and advice, peddling techniques for getting what you want from God. Don't fall for that nonsense. This is your Father you are dealing with, and he knows better than you what you need. With a God like this loving you, you can pray very simply" (Matt. 6:6-9a, *The Message*).

Read Matthew 6:6-9a from the margin. Complete the chart below to compare what God does and does not want from you in prayer.

God Wants	God Doesn't Want

What I want to share with you is rather a way to relate to God that lets us hear Him speak. It's not just a way to wait for Him or to listen to Him or to focus on Him. All those are included, but what I want to share with you is a way of coming to God that delights Him and changes us. It's a way to pray that brings us into union with Him, so that it is no longer we who live but Christ who lives through us. It's a way to know God so well that the deepest desire of His heart actually becomes the deepest desire of ours, and that frees us to ask God for what we really want with confidence that

He'll move heaven and earth to grant our requests because what we want now matches what He wants.

It's the PAPA prayer, and it looks like this:

P: *Present yourself to God without pretense.* Be a real person in the relationship. Tell Him whatever is going on inside you that you can identify.

A: *Attend to how you're thinking of God.* Again, no pretending. Ask yourself, "How am I experiencing God right now?" Is He a vending machine; a frowning father; a distant, cold force? Or is He your gloriously strong but intimate Papa?

P: *Purge yourself of anything blocking your relationship with God.* Put into words whatever makes you uncomfortable or embarrassed when you're real in your relationship with Him. How are you thinking more about yourself and your satisfaction than about anyone else, including God and His pleasure?

A: *Approach God as the "first thing" in your life, as your most valuable treasure, the Person you most want to know.* Admit that other people and things really do matter more to you right now, but you long to want God so much that every other good thing in your life becomes a "second-thing" desire.

That's what I call relational prayer. And I'm coming to see that it belongs in the exact center of my prayer life—for that matter, in the center of my entire spiritual journey. Nothing has relieved my confusion over unanswered prayer requests more than the realization that relational prayer must always come before petitionary prayer. Relate and then request. Enjoy God and then enjoy His provisions, whatever they are.

Just to make sure we've got it, fill in the blanks to review the proper sequence of prayer. ________________ and then ____________________.

Power in petition of God depends on depth of relationship with God. The PAPA prayer is the best way I've discovered to develop and nourish the relationship with God given to me by Jesus through His life, death, and resurrection. Relational prayer provides the Spirit with a wide-open opportunity to do what He loves most to do, to draw me into the heart and life of the Father and to make me more like the Son.

Usually, when I pray the PAPA prayer, nothing happens—at least nothing I can see or feel right away. Sometimes I feel closer to God, or at least I think I do. And sometimes I sense an urge to do something, to reflect on a certain thought, to call a certain person, to think about a certain passage in the Bible, or to read a certain book.

More often, I feel and hear nothing. Praying the PAPA prayer is not rubbing a magic lantern and making known three requests to a docile genie that pops out before our eyes. It's simply a way to come to God and learn to wait, to listen with a little less wax in our spiritual ears, and, most of all, to be relentlessly real.

Read in your Bible Matthew 6:9-13. How does Jesus' Model Prayer reflect the truth that we must relate and then request? ______________________________

Spend a few moments talking honestly with God concerning how you feel about relating with Him as your Papa.

Relational Prayer

Relational Prayer Leads to Personal Transformation

Coming to God in this way creates space in me that the Spirit always fills. Always. I may not know it's happening, but it is. Like nature, the Spirit always fills a vacuum. But we're so busy filling our emptiness, there's not much of a vacuum for Him to fill. That's why narcissists never meet God. They're too busy trying to fill themselves.

As I pray the PAPA prayer, over time I begin to see that my attitude is different. I find myself relating differently with God and with others. I'm a little less into myself, which lets me love better. I ask God for different kinds of things and with a different attitude.

"The PAPA prayer is simply a way to open dialogue with God, to relate with Him more intimately and honestly than I relate with anyone else."
—Larry Crabb

And God, my real Papa, is becoming more real. I can see that I'm on my way to wanting Him more than any other blessing I can imagine. And sometimes, not often, I hear His voice. I'm becoming part of the divine conversation. I'm becoming a participant in the divine nature. And that's union with God.

The PAPA prayer is simply a way to open dialogue with God, to relate with Him more intimately and honestly than I relate with anyone else. It helps me become more interested in listening than speaking, more eager to hear His voice than for Him to hear mine. It's a way of cleaning out my ears so I can become an attentive and discerning listener to God.

And it's a way of surrendering my tongue, that hardest of all beasts to tame (Jas. 3:7-8). It brings together what I most want and what the Father most wants to give. It lets me ask for first things, for what really matters in life, with more eagerness than I ask for second things. I'm coming to see that my health, my family's health, my marriage, my ministry, my bank account, even whether my children are walking with God, are all second things in comparison to the first thing of knowing God, of enjoying Him and trusting Him and serving Him and becoming more like Him.

Read Matthew 6:31-33 in your Bible. What is to take top priority in our lives? ______________________

What happens when we put first things first?

____

The PAPA prayer puts relating with God ahead of asking things from God. It stirs me to value knowing Him more than getting something from Him. And the better I get to know Him, the more I know I'm in for everything my heart could desire, because He loves to make me happy. When I put first things first, I become more confident that second things are on their way. God is running our relationship. It gives Him the first word in our conversation and the last.

"If there were no other advantages, the fact that the PAPA prayer lets me hear His voice would be enough."
—Larry Crabb

Relational Prayer Lets Us Hear God's Voice

If there were no other advantages, the fact that the PAPA prayer lets me hear His voice would be enough. I heard Him just yesterday. I was reading

Jeremiah 32:40-41, "I will never stop doing good to them. … I will rejoice in doing them good … with all my heart and soul."

The Spirit carried those words to my heart. I was overwhelmed with joy. All I could think of was how badly I wanted to make that good news known to others by the way I treated them. A friend who has been driving me crazy came to mind. I wanted to call him, not to point out how he's been annoying me but to do him good.

Once you hear from God, you're hooked. You love your own voice less, and that feels like freedom. You realize you'll never hear a sweeter voice than His, at once infinitely strong and infinitely gentle, the blended voice of the Lion and the Lamb. Listening for that voice becomes what you most want to do. The PAPA prayer is one way to become a listener and to hear what God is saying, and in the process to experience Christ's life coming out of you.

"Guard your steps when you go to the house of God. Go near to listen rather than to offer the sacrifice of fools, who do not know that they do wrong. Do not be quick with your mouth, do not be hasty in your heart to utter anything before God. God is in heaven and you are on earth, so let your words be few" (Eccl. 5:1-2).

Read Ecclesiastes 5:1-2 printed in the margin. Why is it important to become a listener in prayer?__________

This Is No Gimmick— It's a Way to Relate

Prayer is our opportunity to build a passionate relationship with God, to know Him well. True prayer has the power to connect what is deepest in our hearts with what is deepest in His and to release His life into us.

"True prayer has the power to connect what is deepest in our hearts with what is deepest in His and to release His life into us."—Larry Crabb

Read John 15:5-7 in your Bible. Complete this statement: Jesus releases His life in us when we __________.

We ask well of God only if we first relate well with God. We do not relate well with God when we begin our prayers by tuning in to what we want, to what we believe will fulfill our lives and make us happy, and then going to God to ask for it.

Christ's relationship with His Father was the driving passion behind every request He made. Relationship preceded petition. His life is a profound demonstration that getting God is worth infinitely more than getting the things we want *from* God.

Read John 17:20-21. What did Jesus pray for all His followers?
- ❑ **Peace and happiness**
- ❑ **Answered prayers**
- ❑ **Removal from this evil world**
- ❑ **An intimate relationship with God**

I suppose it's clear by now that I am offering the PAPA prayer as a way to develop your relationship with God. But I would rather have you burn this book and warn everyone you meet against it than to have you read it and think the PAPA prayer is a slick gimmick or formula for getting close to God. Nothing we do makes Him do anything. We can only present ourselves to God, attend to our experience of Him, purge ourselves by admitting wrong ways of relating we are powerless to change, and then approach God for mercy. But we want more. We want something that works, that puts us in control, that gives us power to make things happen.

As a result, we are committed to "thing-ism." Come up with a good idea, market the dickens out of it, and pray it becomes the latest thing. Whether it's a new method of prayer or the latest popular author or conference speaker, we love to get on board. Whatever it is, it promises to change our lives. That's the appeal.

Let me speak clearly: I do not recommend the PAPA prayer as a way to make anyone more spiritual. To do so would deny both the Spirit's free sovereignty and our freedom to flow with or resist His movement when it comes. We can make nothing that deeply matters turn out the way we want. So we must keep doing what we can, what we believe we're directed to do, but not to make anything happen. We are to do what's right with a growing awareness of our poverty and dependence. The rest is up to Papa. That's obedience. That's trust. That's humility.

If you have a way to pray that better gets you in touch with your emptiness and God's sufficiency, follow it. But if your prayer life feels like a child sitting on Santa's lap, making a lot of requests of someone you really don't know, then these lessons might be God's message for you.

The PAPA prayer is a way to experience what Jesus had in mind when He said that if we remain in Him and if His Word remains in us, then we could ask for whatever we wanted and He would give it to us.

Revisiting the Questions

One more thing before we start. In the Introduction, on page 108, when I invited you to learn the PAPA prayer, I asked you nine questions to pique your interest—nine questions intended to surface whatever frustration you might be experiencing in your prayer life and to whet your appetite for what a new way to pray could do for your relationship with God.

Let me restate those questions here, rephrasing them a bit:

1. Ever pray for something you didn't receive? Has that become a pattern? ❑ Yes ❑ No

2. Ever seek guidance from the Lord that never came? Does God really guide your decisions? ❑ Yes ❑ No

3. Ever try to convince yourself that you heard from God when you really weren't sure you had? ❑ Yes ❑ No

4. Ever wonder if God even knows what you're going through, let alone cares? ❑ Yes ❑ No

5. Ever feel empty and alone, and then felt more empty and alone after you prayed for comfort? ❑ Yes ❑ No

6. Ever ask for strength to resist temptation and feel the temptation get stronger? ❑ Yes ❑ No

7. Do you enjoy God's company? Do you like to pray just to be with God? ❑ Yes ❑ No

8. Do you think it's possible to enjoy God's company more than you enjoy anyone else's, and do you want to? ❑ Yes ❑ No

9. Do you connect with God in such a way that you hear His voice and know He's with you, no matter what is happening in your life? ❑ Yes ❑ No

I don't want to promise too much. I don't want to stir up hope that will never be realized, but I do want to say this: If you learn the PAPA prayer, if you enter into this opportunity to know God and stick with it, then I believe that what is happening in my life will happen in yours. You will …

- experience new power in petitionary prayer
- receive unmistakable guidance from God
- discover that your soul has "ears" that can hear the voice of God
- enjoy renewed confidence that God is listening to you pray
- know His presence is real
- deepen your appetite for God until you want Him more than any other pleasure
- actually enjoy His company and know He enjoys yours
- yearn to know Him better until knowing Him will become the point of your life
- develop confidence that every empty space in your soul will be filled
- depend on that confidence as your sustaining hope through every trial until you get home

Preparation time is over. Are you ready? Let's learn the PAPA prayer!

"One thing I ask of the LORD, this is what I seek: that I may dwell in the house of the LORD all the days of my life, to gaze upon the beauty of the LORD and to seek him in his temple. My heart says of you, 'Seek his face!' Your face, LORD, I will seek" (Ps. 27:4,8, NIV).

Read Psalm 27:4,8 in the margin. Is the greatest desire of your life to know God intimately?

❑ Yes ❑ No ❑ Not yet

Spend some time being real with God, talking with Him about your greatest desires.

NOTES

To the Leader:

This study challenges readers to be very real with God. Spend time being transparent with God about your prayer life, using the questions in Day 5 as a starting point. Be willing to share your struggles with your class, but also share your hope that God can and will transform your prayer life as you draw closer to Him.

Before the Session

Make a poster of the four steps of the PAPA prayer (p. 112). Display the poster throughout the five weeks of this study.

During the Session

1. Read aloud the nine questions on page 108. Inform participants that if they answered yes to any of those questions then this study of "The PAPA Prayer" is for them. OR Tell participants they have two minutes to get better acquainted with someone in the class. After two minutes, ask: *What did you do to get better acquainted? Did you ask the person to do something for you? to give you something? Why?* Declare that participants will discover through this study of "The PAPA Prayer" that prayer is not a means of getting God to do things for them but of getting better acquainted with God by talking and listening to Him.
2. Inquire: *Is it disconcerting or encouraging to you that Dr. Crabb is very honest about the inadequacy of his prayer life? Why?* Declare that if our prayer lives are going to change, we need to honestly evaluate how we feel about prayer. Request participants silently consider the first activity of Day 1. State that Dr. Crabb is inviting others to join him on his spiritual journey where he learned a richer way to pray. He's not teaching a new formula or gimmick to get God to answer prayers. Ask: *Based on Day 1's title, what does Dr. Crabb feel is the most important aspect of prayer?* Explore why we might not know God very well. Invite someone to read aloud Psalm 42:1-2,11. Ask how the psalmist and Dr. Crabb share the same hope. Declare that participants can know God deeply and that will profoundly impact their prayer lives. Pause for prayer, asking God to teach you to pray.
3. Complete the activities in Day 2. Declare that the PAPA prayer is a way to develop and nourish our relationship with God. Display the poster of the PAPA prayer and go over each step. Inform the group that you will explore each step in detail in the coming weeks.

NOTES

4. Request participants silently read once again the steps of the PAPA prayer and state why they think that type of relational prayer would lead to personal transformation. Discuss the activities in Day 3. Ask: *Why are we hasty to speak to God? How do you listen to God?* Allow volunteers to share instances when they've heard God speak and how that transformed them.
5. Ask: *Does the PAPA prayer mean that prayer is all about relating and not at all about asking?* Allow time for participants to explain their responses. Read the statement from Day 4: "We ask well of God only if we first relate well with God." Invite participants to state why they think that would be so. State that Jesus taught that the power of petitionary prayer depends on the priority of relational prayer. Invite someone to read aloud John 15:5-7. Guide the class to explore what it means to remain in Jesus and what will happen if we do. (Reading this passage from *The Message* might help learners better understand it. You can copy and paste this passage from *www.biblegateway.com.*) Ask: *Is verse 7 a blank check to get anything you want from God? How have people's misunderstandings of this verse caused much confusion and disappointment in prayer? Why must the declaration in verse 7 never be taken out of context but be read with the verses that come before it?* Lead the class to paraphrase verse 7 into an if/then statement that helps them grasp the truth Jesus declared.
6. Explain that the PAPA prayer is one way of remaining in Jesus. Reiterate Dr. Crabb's warning that this is not a gimmick. Explore how people might be tempted to turn the PAPA prayer into a selfish means-to-an-end and how participants can guard against doing so.
7. Request participants prayerfully evaluate their prayer lives using the checklist in Day 5. Invite volunteers to share which of the results of learning to relate with God through the PAPA prayer, listed at the conclusion of Day 5, is the most exciting to them and why. Ask: *In Psalm 27:4,8 how was the psalmist going to achieve his greatest desire?* [Seek.] Declare that we don't find anything without dedication and hard work. Urge participants to commit to seek to know God through this study and the application of the PAPA prayer in their lives.

Present Yourself to God

Stop Trying to Be Who You Think You Should Be

Ed and Melanie are friends of mine. Melanie recently asked me, "How am I supposed to love Ed? He thinks only of himself. I know something's terribly wrong with my attitude. I know I'm bitter, but I really don't know what to do. Sometimes I try to be nicer to him—be warmer, make him a dinner I know he likes. But it never lasts. When I'm nicer, he takes me more for granted. I'm really getting depressed. Any thoughts?"

I replied, "Stop trying to behave the way you think you should."

"Tell him how I really feel? I've tried that too. It makes things worse."

"Pray."

"You think I haven't? I've been on the floor in tears praying about this. But nothing's happening."

"So you're asking God to do something?"

"Yes! To change me. To make me a better wife."

"What would it be like for you to relate to God before you ask Him to change you?"

Pause.

"I have no idea what you're talking about."

My friend Stan has a terrible relationship with his father. Stan's dad has been a functioning alcoholic since before Stan was born—he kept a steady job, made good money, and was a nice enough guy, only occasionally mean. But his kids never felt like he was there.

Stan's mother divorced his father when Stan went away to college. His dad is now on his third marriage. Three months ago, he was diagnosed with advanced prostate cancer. Stan learned about it in an e-mail from his dad's current wife.

"What do I do? I've prayed about it, and I have felt some nudge to go visit him. Maybe the Spirit is leading me to go down there and just love him. I'm not sure. What do you think?"

"First, stop trying to be who you think you should be. Second, as long as you're thinking more about what you should do than about what's going on inside you, I doubt you'll ever clearly hear God's voice leading you."

"So what should I do? I don't understand what you mean about seeing what's going on in me."

"Pray."

"I have. I've prayed every day, asking what God wants me to do. I've even prayed for Dad's salvation. I thought I was getting some direction. Now I'm not so sure."

"That's how you were praying? Asking God for direction?"

"Sure. Something wrong with that?"

"Before you ask God for what you want, it's important to relate to Him." Pause.

"I don't know what you mean."

"I am the vine; you are the branches. If a man remains in me and I in him, he will bear much fruit; apart from me you can do nothing. If anyone does not remain in me, he is like a branch that is thrown away and withers; such branches are picked up, thrown into the fire and burned. If you remain in me and my words remain in you, ask whatever you wish, and it will be given you" (John 15:5-7).

Based on your study of the PAPA prayer and John 15:5-7 last week (see the margin), how would you explain what Dr. Crabb meant to Melanie and Stan?

____

If you want to learn the PAPA prayer, if you want to relate to God before you ask Him for anything, start by presenting yourself to God.

How do you do that? As you get ready to talk with God, tune in to whatever is going on in you—what you're feeling right now, what thoughts are floating through your mind. Tune in to whatever you can identify, and tell God about it. Be real with Him. Hold nothing back. Put into words whatever you know is happening in you.

Check the statement on the top of page 123 with which you would most honestly present yourself to God right now.

- ❑ **You are so far away; right now I'm not even sure You exist.**
- ❑ **I'm so confused and afraid right now. I just don't think I can do this.**
- ❑ **I feel really good right now. Hopeful. Optimistic. Glad to be alive.**
- ❑ **Other: ______________________________**

What would it mean for Stan to present himself to God as the first step in relating to Him before he asks God for guidance? What would it mean for Melanie to come to God by presenting herself as she is to Him in the middle of her marital mess?

What would it mean for you to present yourself before God as you continue to live your life with its mixed assortment of blessings and problems?

It means I would have to be honest with God about

______________________________.

Find Your "Red Dot"

Picture yourself walking into a large shopping mall that you've never been in before. What's the first thing you look for? The directory. When you find it, your eyes scan until you find the red dot that says, "You Are Here." Something in you knows that it's better to fix your location, to get your bearings, before you start looking for where you want to go.

It's the same on the spiritual journey. We need to know where we are before we try to get where we should be.

The Bible teaches that the unobserved life is not worth living.

Read Proverbs 20:5 and Hebrews 4:12 that are printed in the margin. What does God urge us to do?

____

"The purposes of a man's heart are deep waters, but a man of understanding draws them out" (Prov. 20:5).

"For the word of God is living and active. Sharper than any double-edged sword, it penetrates even to dividing soul and spirit, joints and marrow; it judges the thoughts and attitudes of the heart" (Heb. 4:12).

Jesus was really ticked off at the Pharisees for looking at only the outside of their lives, seeing nothing there that particularly concerned them, and then moving on with their religion. "The inside of your life is a dirty mess. Observe that, and then you'll realize that your religion is worthless. It has no power to change you; it only covers up what's wrong." (His actual words are recorded in Matt. 23:25-26, printed in the margin.)

I hear Jesus telling us to take an inside look. See yourself as you really are. Don't take a quick look and then try to change. Reflect on where you are. Talk it over with God. It'll be uncomfortable. But it will make you think more about God. Your focus will shift from yourself to God.

That's what happened in Eden. Adam committed a capital offense against God.

Read Genesis 3:8-10 in your Bible. What did Adam do after he got himself in trouble?______________________

"Woe to you, teachers of the law and Pharisees, you hypocrites! You clean the outside of the cup and dish, but inside they are full of greed and self-indulgence. Blind Pharisee! First clean the inside of the cup and dish, and then the outside also will be clean" (Matt. 23:25-26).

Adam didn't want to stand in his red dot and face God. So he hid behind a tree. Then God showed up for His customary evening stroll and called out, "Adam, where are you?"

Didn't He know? I think God was saying something like this: "Adam, I know where you are. I'm aware of your 'red dot.' But until you come out from hiding, we can't have the relationship we both want. I know you're scared.

"I love you. Stop running away from Me. Stand before Me exactly as you are, with neither defenses nor excuses, and then you'll make the unbelievable discovery that I've come up with a way to welcome you back into a better relationship with Me than you've experienced before or even dreamed possible. You'll need to look deep inside and see what's really going on in you, what you've become, and what terrifies you so much. Then come tell Me about it. I'll take it from there."

The God who invited Adam to take an inside look and present what he saw to God did the same thing with a crowd of people on a Galilean hillside thousands of years later. Jesus was moved by the sight of helpless people hemmed in by problems they couldn't handle and pressured by religious leaders who told them what they should be doing.

"The first step in learning the PAPA prayer is to stop trying to get where we want to go and to be still long enough to see where we are."—Larry Crabb

Read Matthew 11:28-30 in your Bible. What "red dots" did Jesus want the people to acknowledge?

___

Underline the "red dots" you can relate to.

Jesus says, "Come to Me exactly as you are. Stop trying so hard to be good. Admit you're not so good. Admit how disappointed you are in what you've so far experienced of Me. I know you wonder if I even care. Come. Present yourself to Me. It'll be all right. Trust Me."

The first step in learning the PAPA prayer is to stop trying to get where we want to go and to be still long enough to see where we are. But how do we do it? And what can we expect to find when we look inside?

I'll take up those two questions next.

Enter Your Red Dot—Don't Just Describe It

Most of us are afraid to release authentic passion from our hearts, to put into words what is deepest within us.

My father was an emotionally alive but suppressed man. We loved each other, but we shared very few moments of real encounter. One time, James Dobson interviewed both of us after the publication of the book we wrote together, *God of My Father.*

In the middle of the interview, Dr. Dobson leaned toward Dad and said, "Mr. Crabb, you must be very proud of your son." I struggled to maintain my composure. My father had never put into words that he loved me or was proud of me. I waited, not sure if I was stretched out on a guillotine or about to be crowned.

Dad shifted in his chair. Then he spoke. "Well, we have to be careful not to get big heads, but yes, God has used Larry in a variety of ways."

That was it. The blade dropped. It's been hard to get my big head back in place. At that moment, I would have given anything to see Dad beam and to hear him say, "Dr. Dobson, if I had my choice of any man in history, I'd have chosen Larry for my son." I believe he could have said those words and meant them. The passion I longed to hear was in him, but he didn't enter his "red dot." Why?

Why do most of us, even the emotionally expressive among us who easily say, "I love you" and "I think the world of you," so rarely speak from our depths? Why do most of us never even realize there are unexplored depths within us, let alone enter them?

"When Jesus had finished saying these things, the crowds were amazed at his teaching, because he taught as one who had authority, and not as their teachers of the law" (Matt. 7:28-29).

When our Lord spoke, people knew that something about His words was radically different. What was it? As you read the Scriptures in the margin, underline what made the difference.

"The people were amazed at his teaching, because he taught them as one who had authority" (Mark 1:22).

Jesus spoke with authority. He spoke from the center of His being. He knew who He was in His core and was comfortable in being exactly who He knew Himself to be. He was the most, the only, authentic person who ever lived. He was familiar with the depths within Him, and He always spoke out of those depths in ways that suited His God-honoring purposes.

Why aren't we more authentic? What keeps us more social than real? Do we fear that if we were real, we would run from others in terror of rejection or run toward them in pathetic neediness or maybe in violent hatred? Was Freud right? Do we have to somehow keep our desires in check while at the same time indulge enough of them to keep us reasonably happy?

Why was my father so afraid to say what was in his heart? Why do I have the same struggle? Could I learn to be more authentic, at least with God, to present myself before Him in my red dot?

It's important that I do. It's important for you as well. Without presenting ourselves to God, without entering our red dot and speaking authentically from whatever is there, we will never develop the relationship with Him that we long for, that He longs for, that we could enjoy together.

Read Psalm 25:1-2,11-17 in your Bible.
Record words or phrases that demonstrate David presented himself authentically to God.

____

Record words or phrases that demonstrate the resulting relationship with God.

____

What keeps us from getting real with God? Let me address that question first. The other question, how to get real, I'll respond to next.

Our Deepest Longing and Our Worst Terror

Most of us live life on its surface. We may think we've gone beneath, but we've not reached our center until we've faced and felt a longing that nothing in this world can satisfy. More than anything else, we yearn to be in a relationship where the love we receive defines our identity and the meaning we live for defines our value, where we can then live as the unique people we are, following the unique calling on our lives.

"More than anything else, we yearn to be in a relationship where the love we receive defines our identity and the meaning we live for defines our value, where we can then live as the unique people we are, following the unique calling on our lives."
—Larry Crabb

Complete this statement: More than anything else in this life, I want ______________________________ .

Because we intuitively sense that something about us is difficult to accept, something worse than what we do, something terrible that defines who we are, we intuitively sense our need to relate with someone who can forgive us and envision who we could become.

That desire is shared by men and women. A man's fear is this: Am I adequate? Do I have the weight to handle important tasks, to impact a woman, a child, a friend, in a way that affirms my value? A man's deepest terror is weightlessness, the absence of solid substance that others recognize and appreciate.

A woman's fear is this: Am I beautiful, or am I merely useful? a sexual object? a resource that functions well to achieve another's purpose? The flip side of desire is terror. Can I connect deeply with anyone? Is anyone safe? Will anyone see my beauty, or is there nothing to see?

Let's go deep here. What is your greatest fear?
- ❑ **I'm unlovable.**
- ❑ **I don't measure up.**
- ❑ **I have no purpose.**
- ❑ **I have no beauty.**
- ❑ **Other: ____________________________________**

With fallen ingenuity, we handle our terror by shoving our deepest longings out of awareness and assuming control over lesser ones. With terror numbed, we live to protect ourselves. We find a relational style that keeps us feeling pretty good, and when something threatens to arouse our deep pain and terror, we retreat or attack. We do whatever it takes to keep ourselves intact. Our red dot of unsatisfied desire and consuming terror stays hidden.

Dad did what all men do. He let his terror of weightlessness get in the way of pouring his masculine depth into my starving soul. I struggle with the same problem as a husband, dad, friend, and counselor. I struggle to present the emptiness of my unsatisfied desire and the controlling power of my consuming terror to God. So do Melanie and Stan.

My word to Melanie and Stan, and to you and to me, is this: If you never enter your red dot, you'll never discover the God whose love displaces terror. And you'll never discover the real you, the wonderful you that's strong and beautiful, weighty and desirable. You'll never find yourself until you find God in your red dot or until He finds you in your brokenness.

"There is no fear in love. But perfect love drives out fear" (1 John 4:18).

Read 1 John 4:18, printed in the margin. Use this prayer starter to begin a dialogue with God. "Father, Papa, I don't want to be afraid anymore ... "

How to Enter Your Red Dot

If something is stirring within you, if you feel a desire to enter your internal world of reality and present yourself to God, then consider three suggestions.

First, make a lifestyle of reflection on your red dot. No, I'm not suggesting you get obsessed about it. Eat your lunch and call your friend and go to work without always wondering what's happening in your depths. But yes, I am suggesting that you take a break a few times every day. Spend a few minutes asking yourself, "What am I aware of going on in me right now? What am I feeling? What am I wishing would happen? What am I scared of?"

When you wake up at 2:00 in the morning, don't immediately grab a book or switch on the TV or take a pill. Lie there and reflect on what's stirring in your heart and mind. Tell God about it. Call Him Papa.

Read Psalm 139:1-4 in your Bible. Why is going to God the perfect action to take when you're seeking to enter your red dot?__________________________

Don't expect that a one-time effort to face where you are will strike pay dirt. Make it a lifestyle. A few minutes every day. Reflect on what's going on in you as you pick up your Bible or open your devotional book. Make a lifestyle of reflecting on your red dot. It will help you know what's going on inside you when you present yourself to God.

Second, pay attention to your dreams. No, I'm not a Jungian or a Freudian, but especially vivid dreams that you clearly remember the next morning sometimes express hidden conflict you've purposefully hidden. If you're going to present more and more of yourself to God, use various opportunities (like dreams) to peek into the world of your thoughts and feelings.

Just last night, I dreamed that I was at the gym, bench-pressing a weight I normally handle easily, when my arms went limp and the barbell crashed into my chest, broke my ribcage, and I was rushed to the hospital.

If you desire to dig deeper ...

Read the following passages in your Bible. What longings or fears were addressed in these dreams?

Genesis 15: __________

Genesis 28: __________

Daniel 2,4: __________

Matthew 1:18-24 ____
____

Acts 18:1-11: ________
____

I thought about my dream this morning. A heavy speaking schedule is on the horizon, dozens of e-mails await my response, a desire to enjoy my family gnaws at me, and a couple of big deadlines are closing in.

As I visualized the barbell falling and my arms having no power to resist the impact, I could feel the terror that I'd be exposed as an imposter. I'm not a man. I'm a little boy. I have no strength. All these years I've been pretending. I can't handle all that's on my plate. Why pretend?

I awoke at 4 a.m. this morning. I spent half an hour talking this over with God. I presented myself, stirred by the dream. I was at my desk by 5:30 a.m., writing. It felt good. I felt alive again, sweating and moving ahead like a man, lifting heavy weights with ease.

Third, follow the "affective track" in the presence of a trusted friend. Affect simply means emotion. Stay on the lookout for distinct feelings that arise within you. They may be ugly emotions like perverted lust or violent anger. They may be glorious emotions such as an exhilarating sense of freedom or joy. Or they might just be everyday emotions, like impatience with rude drivers or pleasure in a good cup of coffee.

Tune in. Meditate on what you feel. See your affect as a doorway opening in front of you. Walk through it. See where it leads. Don't analyze. Don't try to see what your emotions mean or where they come from. Simply flow with them. Follow their lead.

Talk about your affective red dot with a friend. Getting real with a trusted friend will make it easier to get real with God and to feel His love.

"But God demonstrates his own love for us in this: While we were still sinners, Christ died for us... For if, when we were God's enemies, we were reconciled to him through the death of his Son, how much more, having been reconciled, shall we be saved through his life!" (Rom. 5:8,10).

Reread Proverbs 20:5, printed in the margin of Day 2. Who might be your "person of understanding" who can draw out your deepest thoughts?____________

Present yourself to God. He'll present Himself to you. That's the first step in the PAPA prayer.

Read Romans 5:8,10, printed in the margin (or Rom. 5:6-10 in your Bible). Why is it safe to present yourself honestly to God? ____________________

NOTES

To the Leader:

Meditate on Psalm 139 this week. Allow the psalmist's honesty before God to encourage and guide you to present yourself to God just as you are with all your fears and longings.

Before the Session

1. Cut a large circle out of a red poster board and write on it "You Are Here." Display the circle in a prominent location.
2. Secure a copy of *The Baptist Hymnal,* 1991 edition.

During the Session

1. Draw attention to the red dot. Ask: *Do you think it is always necessary to know where you are in order to get where you want to be? Explain. How does that relate to our spiritual journey?* Declare that we need to truthfully acknowledge where we are with God before we can move forward in our relationship with Him. OR Organize the class into two groups. Instruct Group 1 to read Melanie's story from Day 1 and answer the first activity as it relates to Melanie. Request Group 2 to read Stan's story and answer the first activity. Allow groups time to share.
2. Ask the class to imagine they are trying to tune their radio to a Christian station. Ask what it takes to move from static to their favorite preacher or praise song. [Samples: It takes some adjustments, patience, etc.] Ask: *What happens if you never tune in? What happens if you do?* Encourage participants to have patience to make adjustments in their lives so they can tune in to what is going on inside them, present themselves to God, and have a vibrant prayer life. Without getting too personal, discuss how participants can complete the statement at the conclusion of Day 1.
3. Invite someone to read aloud Matthew 23:25-28. Lead a discussion with: *Why did Jesus pronounce judgment on the Pharisees? What did He charge them to do? What "red dots" would they have had to acknowledge if they truly were going to relate to God?* Explore why Dr. Crabb urges, "Don't take a quick look and then try to change."
4. Request a volunteer read aloud Genesis 3:6-10. Inquire: *Do you think God's question was for His sake or for Adam's sake? Explain. What did Adam have to lose by hiding from God? What did he have to gain by being honest about where he was and why?* Discuss the last

NOTES

activity of Day 2. Request someone read the quotation in the margin of Day 2. Ask why that advice is so difficult to follow. Read Psalm 46:10 from the *New International Version* or from the *King James Version.* Examine: *What do we discover when we're still? What will we discover about ourselves when we begin to fully know that the Lord is God?*

5. Relate Dr. Crabb's story about his father from Day 3. Ask his questions: *Why aren't we more authentic? What keeps us more social than real?* Discuss the first activity of Day 3. Explore how we can speak with more authenticity. Complete the final activity of Day 3.
6. Ask participants how they think most people would complete these statements: "More than anything else in this life I want ... " "More than anything else in this life I fear ... " Inquire: *How did Dr. Crabb say we handle our terror? Do you tend to retreat or attack when your deepest fears are exposed? Why do we need to "enter our red dot" even if it initially causes us to feel threatened or vulnerable?* Ask someone to read aloud 1 John 4:18. Evaluate why perfect love drives away fear. Allow volunteers to share how that has been true in their lives.
7. Discuss the first activity of Day 5. Contrast the difference between becoming obsessed with your red dot and making a lifestyle of reflection on your red dot. Allow participants to state whether the idea of paying attention to dreams makes them uncomfortable and why. Read Job 33:14-17. State that since the Bible declares God speaks through dreams, we would do well to pay attention to our dreams. Invite volunteers who completed the "Dig Deeper" activity in the margin on page 129 to share what they discovered.
8. Determine why it's important to find a friend with whom one can be real. Ask someone to read aloud Proverbs 20:5. Explore how class participants can be "persons of understanding" for one another. Discuss the final activity of Day 5. Encourage participants: *Since God has already seen you at your worst and loves you anyway, you can be free and safe to honestly present yourself to God.* For your closing prayer, read the words to "Just As I Am" (No. 307, *The Baptist Hymnal,* 1991).

Attend to How You Are Thinking of God

Your Picture of God

What picture of God comes to mind when you pray? Who do you assume He is? What's He like? What conception of God is already in you that, perhaps beneath your awareness, rumbles around when you talk to Him?

The second step in learning the PAPA prayer is to attend to who you think you're talking to when you pray and then to correct whatever misrepresentation becomes clear. As you work through this step, you may realize you have no idea who God is. No picture emerges. No image comes to mind.

That might be a good thing. Sometimes we pray most meaningfully when we have no sense that He is present or even exists. It's then that deliberate faith, a strong act of the will, carries our prayers. Life can get so dark that we must draw on the kind of faith that stubbornly continues to hang on to what we once knew was true.

"Now faith is being sure of what we hope for and certain of what we do not see. This is what the ancients were commended for. By faith we understand that the universe was formed at God's command, so that what is seen was not made out of what was visible" (Heb. 11:1-3).

What is commendable according to Hebrews 11:1-3?

____

When You Have No Picture of God

Many of us have had moments when we were overwhelmed by an unmistakable sense of God's presence, and, in those moments, lifting Him to first place in our affections seemed natural.

We are never more fully who we really are than when we follow God whether we experience Him or not. Faith that believes when it cannot see releases our true identity; it weakens both the defenses that blur that identity and the self-serving passions that too often rule our choices.

Read 1 Peter 1:8 in your Bible and complete the statement: Even though I can't see God, I can still

____.

Don't worry if no picture of God or clear idea of who He is comes to mind when you pray. You may be in a place that leads into the richest communion with Him.

When You Have a False Picture of God

Most of us, however, see something. Some idea of God is fixed in our minds that comes less from a direct revelation of God and more from early encounters with church and our earthly dads.

I asked one person who she visualized God to be as she talked to Him, and she quickly replied, "A pygmy in a wheelchair." I hadn't heard that one before, so I asked what that image symbolized. "I sometimes feel like I'm talking to an undersized person who's too disabled, though He means well, to do much of anything."

"Whatever idea of God is in your mind as you talk with Him will influence the way you pray." —Larry Crabb

Another said, "I really hadn't paid attention to it before, but I think I picture God as an angry white-haired man with a flowing robe, outstretched arms, and fire coming out of His eyes."

I read her John's description of Jesus in the first chapter of Revelation. She said, "That's Him!" I suspect the painting of Moses throwing down the tablets of stone in a rage shaped her image as well.

How do you picture God when you pray? Whatever idea of God is in your mind as you talk with Him will influence the way you pray. It's possible that millions of Christians across the world who think they're praying in Jesus' name are in fact praying in the name of someone else, to a God the Bible knows nothing of.

Ten Common Images of God

I've identified 10 common images of God that are in people's minds when they pray. The Bible won't let us pin God down to one image that we can get comfortable with. The more we read, the deeper the mystery becomes.

Job 11:7-8 asks several probing questions. As you read the verses below, write your answer beside each question.
"Can you fathom the mysteries of God?" ________
"Can you probe the limits of the Almighty?" ________
"They are higher than the heavens—what can you do?" ________
"They are deeper than the depths of the grave—what can you know?" ________

We want to know who it is we're talking to when we pray. We hate mystery. We like control, or at least predictability. So we come up with images that serve our purposes. Here are brief descriptions of those images.

1. *Smiling Buddy.* He's there for you the way a good friend should be. Immanence without transcendence, with us but not above us—a God who just likes hanging out. No demands. No rules. Just a good time. Think of God as a smiling buddy, and prayer will become nothing more than asking favors from a chum.

2. *Backroom Watchmaker.* This is the way I often misperceive God. I sometimes feel alone in an indifferent universe, designed and wound up to keep ticking by a craftsman who never leaves the shop. He made the clock. Now He has other things to do. I prayed for my brother's safe flight the day his plane crashed. Why bother with prayer? The clock keeps ticking.

3. *Preoccupied King.* We picture God as preoccupied with more important matters. He's absorbed with evangelism, crusades, political battles over

abortion, and which church plant will become the next megachurch. Our prayers feel small, petty, not worthy of our preoccupied king's attention.

4. *Vending Machine.* Just put in the coins and collect your treat. We pray. It works. The parking spot opened up. The lump disappeared. The new job came. Let's pray more. Let's insert more coins. God is good.

5. *Stern Patriarch.* This one often develops out of experience with religious fathers or legalistic churches. Carry the biggest Bible you can find. Walk away when someone uses a bad word. Place your napkin on your lap when you sit for dinner. God can be obeyed but not enjoyed. Prayer is stiff, rigid. Worship lacks passion. Petitions are offered in a shy voice.

6. *Kindly Grandfather.* Prayers to a kindly grandfather sound like the whiny pleadings of an insufferably adorable child. A little girl hugs your neck. A little boy playfully pokes your arm. "OK, you can have candy before dinner. But just one piece. Well, maybe two."

7. *Impersonal Force.* This is the "blank stare" image of God. This idea of God is a power that cannot be harnessed. It's the image of an impersonal force straight from Star Wars. God is more a thing than a person. Prayer, at best, might redirect the flow of electricity, but it never connects you to someone who loves you.

8. *Cruel Tyrant.* It's hard at times not to see God as cruel. He directed Satan's attention to Job, a good man, and then turned the Devil loose to torture him. And when you doubt His goodness, sin seems eminently reasonable. Why not? Find a little pleasure in a world run by a God who has no interest in looking out for you. Is that so wrong?

9. *Moral Crusader.* What God hates most are visible sins, the sins of culture—abortion, pornography, gambling, same-sex marriage, and adultery, to name a few. Personal spiritual formation is a secondary concern. Turning the national tide back to God is the first thing. Mobilize resources and raise money. Devote your best spiritual energy to praying about the things that matter most.

10. *Romantic Lover.* God loves us, as individuals. He longs to satisfy our hearts, to communicate how profoundly He loves us so we can feel valuable, special, and cherished. Center your life on pursuing the experience of deep connection to God. Whatever comes into your life that provides an experience of ecstasy, of soul connection, thank God for it. Whatever creates misery, run from it, into the arms of your Lover.

How do you picture God when you pray? Either check one of the ten images discussed today or describe your own image of God in the margin.

Next time you talk to God, step back for a minute and ask yourself, "Who do I think I'm talking to?"

Who Has God Shown Himself to Be?

Read the following Scriptures in your Bible. Draw a line from each reference to the statement it makes about Jesus.

John 12:44-45	**Jesus is the image of the invisible God.**
John 14:9	**To look at Jesus is to see God.**
Colossians 1:15	**Jesus is the exact representation of God.**
Hebrews 1:3	**Anyone who has seen Jesus has seen God.**

If we want to know who the Father is, what He's like, we can look at Jesus. The visible Son is a mirror image of the invisible Father. Today we're going to take a close look at Jesus as He is right now, in order to get a clear picture of God, of the Papa we're talking to when we pray.

Praying to God is something like e-mailing a relative you've never met, who lives in a place you've never been. In return correspondence (to embellish the analogy), your relative never sends a picture of himself, never sends a picture of his house or land, and always writes a generic letter addressed to "My much loved relatives," like the ones we receive every Christmas.

His e-mails never come only to you and are therefore never addressed only to you. He never calls. And you can't call him. He has no phone.

It would be nearly impossible to not imagine what this person we've never seen looks like. We ask. He never replies. So we give up all hope of forming a clear picture of what our relative looks like or where he lives.

We become aware, however, that what we really want is to know him. What's he like? What would he be like to be with? Now that we've moved past the surface stuff, we're curious about what matters.

Maybe that's why the Bible tells us so little of the kinds of things we usually want to know about someone we've never met. We're intended to move past the social matters to the personal. Who is this God we pray to?

I'm not sure if, until recently, I've ever asked personal questions about God, if I've ever thought hard about who He is and how it would feel to be with Him. I think I've assumed I already knew.

Without troubling my head about it, I've assumed God was the cosmic craftsman, the backroom watchmaker who made the world, set its gears in place, and then let it tick away. At other times, I've preferred to see Him as my romantic lover whom I have every right to expect will satisfy me.

"Real spiritual maturity . . . enjoys God's delightful unpredictability."
—Lawrence Crabb, Sr.

It occurs to me that I may have had my clearest, most accurate glimpses of God when He was most obscure, most mysterious, and uncategorizable. My father loved to say that real spiritual maturity means to enjoy God's delightful unpredictability.

I've never expected to literally see God, ever. Perhaps in heaven Papa will somehow be visible to us, but I doubt it. I know I'll see Jesus, and I think then I'll understand His words, "Anyone who has seen me has seen the Father" (John 14:9). I'll be content with that. Fully satisfied. Delirious.

But what about now? I don't see Papa. I don't see Jesus. I don't see the Spirit. What picture, if any, am I to form of Papa when I talk to Him?

God doesn't send a photo album replete with snapshots of Him talking to Abraham or of Jesus driving out vendors from the temple.

What did God give to help us know Him that's even better than a photo album? ____________________

God has compiled a collection of pictures-in-narrative, none that reduce Him to one comfortable image but a scrapbook filled with stories.

Some of them disturb us, but when we enter them deeply enough, they powerfully draw us toward Him.

He includes a final few pages of images. Images reach deeper than stories, certainly deeper than didactic teaching. When the Spirit wanted to finish the Bible, He wrote Revelation, the unveiling of Jesus Christ through images. No other book as clearly and compellingly creates an image of God that we can—and should—picture when we pray. We'll never see our Papa, but we can see Him in Jesus.

As you read the next few pages, attend to God. Is the image that's presented different from the way you've pictured God?

A Vision of the Risen Christ

John, the writer of Revelation, had been exiled to the prison camp of Patmos for treason. He was viewed as both an atheist and an enemy of the state. John was left to die on the island of Patmos.

Here's how he greeted his friends in a letter: "I, John, your brother and companion in the suffering and kingdom and patient endurance that are ours in Jesus, was on the island of Patmos because of the word of God and the testimony of Jesus" (Rev. 1:9).

I think I might have mentioned that my suffering was more than theirs and that my need for patient endurance was far greater than theirs.

Read Revelation 1:10 in your Bible. What did John do in his exile?
❑ Complain
❑ Send out an SOS
❑ Worship God

John was looking not at his circumstances but at his Lord.

And then it happened. Jesus Christ appeared to him. Remember, John was the one who 60 years earlier, over dinner, had rested his head comfortably on Jesus' chest.

Not long afterward, John watched Jesus writhe in agony on the cross. When John later pastored the church at Ephesus, he brought Mary, the mother of Jesus, with him to the fellowship, looking after her as Jesus had requested. He had last seen Jesus, still in the form of an ordinary man, after His resurrection, talking with John and his friends, and then lifting off the ground and floating into the clouds and out of their sight.

Had you asked John who he visualized when he prayed, I suppose it would have been one of those images. Any one would have been wonderful. But after the vision he received on Patmos, his image of Christ was never the same. It couldn't have been.

Read Revelation 1:12-16 for a description of what John actually saw. In the margin, draw the outline of a man. On the outline, sketch or write the details of Jesus that John observed.

John had seen the transfigured Christ, but he had never seen anything like this. No doubt he had sensed God's presence on Patmos many times. But now his Papa gave John a vision of Jesus Christ as He was then and is today. My guess is that his prayers at the end of his life were exquisitely rich.

"I heard behind me a voice like a trumpet." Perhaps John's mind went to the apostle Paul's words, that the Lord's second coming would be announced by a trumpet (1 Thess. 4:16). John must have thought, *Something big is happening. Someone huge is coming.*

"I turned … I saw… someone 'like a son of man.' " Hundreds of years before, Daniel had been given a vision of "one like a son of man. … He approached the Ancient of Days" (Dan. 7:13). The term "son of man" refers to the most important person in all history. In the ancient Near East, it was perhaps the most pretentious title anyone could have used. In other words, John is saying, "So, it's Him! It's Jesus Christ I am seeing. No one matters more in all the universe or here on Patmos."

"Dressed in a robe reaching down to his feet and with a golden sash around his chest." The robe of a priest was on Jesus, and the sash was around his chest. When a man was preparing to work, he fastened the sash around his waist, so the flowing material wouldn't get in his way. When his work was finished, he lifted the sash around his chest.

Jesus is our priest, our bridge between man and God, the highway into Papa's presence. The sash is around His chest. The work is done. We can now stride boldly into the throne room of heaven. It's where we belong.

Read John 19:28-30, printed in the margin. Spend time in prayer, thanking Jesus for finishing the work so you can have an intimate relationship with God.

"Later, knowing that all was now completed, and so that the Scripture would be fulfilled, Jesus said, 'I am thirsty.' A jar of wine vinegar was there, so they soaked a sponge in it, put the sponge on a stalk of the hyssop plant, and lifted it to Jesus' lips. When he had received the drink, Jesus said, 'It is finished.' With that, he bowed his head and gave up his spirit" (John 19:28-30).

We'll pick up here tomorrow and talk more about the risen Christ.

A Vision of the Risen Christ (Part 2)

"His head and hair were white like wool, as white as snow." John no doubt flipped through the pages of his mind to Isaiah 1:18: "Though your sins are like scarlet, they shall be as white as snow; though they are red as crimson, they shall be like wool." Jesus Christ is ageless, wise beyond all the elders, and utterly pure. And John was seeing Him. That meant death, unless by some miracle John too had been declared pure, clean, undefiled.

"'But,' he said, 'you cannot see my face, for no one may see me and live'" (Ex. 33:20).

John was saying, "I am standing in His holy presence. With Him, I am forever alive, and will share in the wisdom of the ages."

"His eyes were like blazing fire." Nothing changes the human heart so deeply as to look bad in the presence of love, to be seen with all that is wickedly ugly about us and still be wanted, to be delighted in. That's grace.

We live to pretend, to hide what is bad and parade what is good. It prevents community from becoming grace-based and real. And it keeps us from enjoying God. But John told us, "He sees me. He sees everything. My sin is still with me. But He remains! Can it be?"

"She [Hagar] gave this name to the LORD who spoke to her: 'You are the God who sees me,' for she said, 'I have now seen the One who sees me'" (Gen. 16:13).

Read Genesis 16:13, printed in the margin. What does it mean to you that you can pray to a God whose name is "the God who sees me"? ____________________

"His feet were like bronze glowing in a furnace." Jesus's feet were fire-tested bronze. With all its flaws, the church will never disappear. Jesus can carry our weight, all of it, from the medieval Inquisition to the last church split. John was saying, "I am your companion in the kingdom of Christ. Neither external persecution nor internal pressure can destroy my real home."

"His voice was like the sound of rushing waters." I have stood at the base of Niagara Falls. The sound of rushing water is at once deafening and soothing. It blocks out all other noise and quiets my heart. As John said, "I hear nothing but Him! And my soul is at rest."

"In his right hand he held seven stars." The stars Jesus held were the angels assigned to each of the seven churches. No star is running things. Jesus is in charge. John assured us, "He is in control. I am safe from whatever would harm my soul. My body they may kill. His truth abideth still. I am secure."

"You become yourself by knowing [Papa] as He really is." —Larry Crabb

"Out of his mouth came a sharp two-edged sword." The sword referred to is not the long blade of the fencer. It is rather a curved, short blade used to plunge into someone at close range.

Jesus gets up close and personal, like a surgeon. His eyes see what's wrong more clearly than the most sensitive MRI. And He cuts with a precision every surgeon would envy.

"His face was like the sun shining in all its brilliance." One more time John remembered his Old Testament. "The Lord bless you and keep you; the Lord make his face shine upon you and be gracious to you; the Lord turn his face toward you and give you peace" (Num. 6:24-26). No blessing was greater to a Jew. John must have been thrilled.

Read Revelation 1:17 in your Bible. Record the actions each took and why:

John ______________________________

Jesus ______________________________

When John stood up after his encounter with the risen Lord, I suspect he was more fully John than ever before. Why? Knowing Papa does that to you. You become yourself by knowing Him as He really is.

Let me ask you to attend to your experience of God. Then change it, deliberately, consciously, every time you pray, to match the image of Revelation 1. That's step two in learning the PAPA prayer.

NOTES

To the Leader:

Bible study leader, how do you picture God when you pray? You don't have to have a perfectly clear image of God, but you need to be striving to move deeper in your relationship with Him so He becomes increasingly clearer to you. Displayed growth in your own relationship with God is what will really teach the adults in your Bible study class.

Before the Session

1. Secure a large box and place it in the center of your meeting space.
2. Secure an empty picture frame.

During the Session

1. Ask: *How do you picture God when you pray?* OR Draw attention to the large box in the center of the room. Discuss how people try to put God in a box and why. FOR EITHER OPTION Ask: *Does it even matter what image of God you have when you pray as long as you pray to Him? Why?* On the PAPA Prayer poster you displayed during the first session of this study, point out the first "A" and ask participants to read together the second step (or the title of Week 3). Today's lesson will help participants gain a correct biblical concept of God.
2. Display the picture frame and state that many people's picture frame of God is empty. Evaluate why not having a picture of God is not necessarily a bad thing. Discuss the two activities of Day 1. Invite volunteers to share how it is possible that a deeper intimacy with God can grow out of times when they have no sense of the One to whom they are praying.
3. Declare that a greater problem than not having a mental image of God is having a false picture of God. Ask someone to read the last statement of Day 1. Allow participants to state why they agree or disagree. Ask: *If millions of Christians aren't even praying to the God of the Bible, what does that say about the power of the church's prayers? What must we do with our false images of God if we want to pray with power and intimacy?*
4. If possible, organize the class into five small groups or pairs. Assign each group 2 of the 10 common images of God described in Day 2. Instruct the small groups to be prepared to share with the larger group a description of the two common images of God they were assigned and tell why each image does not lead to true prayer. After several moments, call on each group to share. Ask participants which images they think are completely off the mark and which images portray

NOTES

at least a slight reflection of God's true image. Hold up the empty picture frame and ask: *Do you think we could ever put a complete picture of God in this frame? Why?* Request the class answer aloud as you read the four questions asked in Job 11:7-8 [the first activity of Day 2]. Inquire: *Why should those truths comfort and encourage us in our prayer lives rather than frighten or discourage us?*

5. State: *You can't put God in a box. You can't fit God into a frame. What's the only thing that contains an accurate image of God?* [Refer adults to the second activity of Day 3.] State that we see many different images of God throughout Scripture—some are pleasant and some are disturbing; all give a glimpse into the nature of God. As time permits, ask volunteers to read the following passages: Exodus 33:12-23; Numbers 21:4-9; Mark 10:13-16; John 2:13-17. After each passage, discuss whether the image of God portrayed was comforting or disturbing and why. Explore why the characteristic of God displayed in that passage adds to the overall portrait of God. Ask why passages about Jesus can guide the class to gain a glimpse into the image of God. Discuss the first activity of Day 3.
6. State that John's vision of Jesus in the Book of Revelation is perhaps the most vivid image of God portrayed in Scripture. Invite someone to read aloud Revelation 1:9-10. Ask when Jesus appeared to John. [When he worshiped.] Allow volunteers to share how Jesus becomes more real to them during times of worship. Request someone read aloud Revelation 1:12-18. [If you are *really* brave, or a really good artist, put your artistic rendering of this passage from the second activity of Day 4 into the picture frame.]
7. Using Dr. Crabb's comments in Days 4 and 5, discuss the significance of each phrase in Revelation 1:10-16 and explore how that helps participants gain a fuller image of the God to whom they pray. Ask: *How can attending to this image of God transform your relationship with Him and consequently your prayer life?* Read Dr. Crabb's challenge in the last paragraph of Day 5. Determine ways participants can follow his suggestions. Use the prayer activity at the conclusion of Day 4 on the top of page 141 as your closing prayer.

Purge Yourself of Anything That Blocks Your Relationship with God

Who Do You Turn to When You're Scared?

What I'm about to say is either a bunch of sweet words that have as much nourishing value as a Twinkie, or it's one of the most staggering and under-appreciated truths in the Bible.

In the center of your soul and mine, the Shekhinah glory resides—the literal, real, overwhelming presence of God. And when we live out of that center, all the self-seeking, self-serving energy that guides so much of what we think and feel and do, often without even knowing it, is miraculously displaced by love.

Shekhinah glory: The literal, real, overwhelming presence of God.

If that's true, then we have no choice but to admit we don't usually live out of that center. Something's getting in the way, blocking our access to it, leaving us in the control of that miserable, self-obsessed energy that we so easily mistake as necessary, even Christian.

I can think of nothing I want more than to enter the "sanctuary of the center," this holy place that is already in us where we can have communion with God.

Read Psalm 25:14 in your Bible. What did David declare happens when we're in this sanctuary?

- ❑ **All our problems disappear.**
- ❑ **We feel better about ourselves.**
- ❑ **We convince God to accept us.**
- ❑ **God confides in us.**

I long to join that conversation. I want to sit on the floor with Papa or go for a long walk with His arm resting on my shoulder and listen to Him tell me His secret thoughts, share with me His deepest feelings, and let me in on what He's doing and what He wants to do through me.

I want to hear Him express His love for me in ways my earthly father never could. And I want to be heard by Him, to know He knows all that I'm going through. I want to feel His life, His substance, stirring in me and released from me, to know that I'm neither invisible nor weightless; that I've been fully seen and am still wanted, fully wanted; that I'm being sent on a mission I've been equipped to handle, a mission that matters. I want to find myself in finding Him. I want to be released to be who I am in Christ.

And it's possible. It's available to me. What I want the most I can have. For one reason: God Himself is in me.

What would you most like to discover in an intimate conversation with God?____________________________

Papa's Spirit has moved into my heart and made it His home. Every minute He's whispering that Jesus loves me. He tells me every day that I'm one of a kind, equipped as no one else in the history of time to advance His kingdom in unique ways that no one else has ever been asked to do. The Spirit in me is carrying Papa's voice into my heart, where I can hear it.

But most of us don't hear it, not always, sometimes not at all. Why not?

Read Psalm 25:11 in your Bible. What word clues us into a key reason we don't hear Papa's voice? ________

Purge Yourself of Your Relational Sin

We don't hear God's Spirit in our hearts because something's getting in the way. As we pour out everything in us to God (presenting), and as we more clearly see who we're talking to when we pray (attending), two things will happen. We'll become even more aware of how intensely we want to get close to God, and we'll realize how stubbornly and foolishly we resist it.

"Any true experience of God is given, not achieved."
—Larry Crabb

There's a third thing that will happen. We'll feel impotent and humbled. We'll realize we have no power to make this relationship with God be all we want it to be, that any true experience of God is given, not achieved; and we'll see that our part in making ourselves available for this relationship involves our willingness to recognize and confess the obstacles we have created between ourselves and our Papa.

Read Psalm 25:16-18 in your Bible and note what David
1. Recognized about himself: ______________________

2. Confessed he needed: ______________________

"You, therefore, have no excuse, you who pass judgment on someone else, for at whatever point you judge the other, you are condemning yourself, because you who pass judgment do the same things. Now we know that God's judgment against those who do such things is based on truth. So when you, a mere man, pass judgment on them and yet do the same things, do you think you will escape God's judgment? Or do you show contempt for the riches of his kindness, tolerance and patience, not realizing that God's kindness leads you toward repentance?" (Rom. 2:1-4).

Here's where we run headlong into the problem of self-deception. We're blind to our worst faults. We can see what's wrong with everybody else (especially our spouse and kids and friends and pastors), but we can't see—we don't want to see—what's wrong with us.

And it's not because nothing much is wrong. It's easy for us to say, "Well, I know I make mistakes; after all, I'm no saint, but ..." and then go on to enjoyably point out the flaws in others.

Read Romans 2:1-4, printed in the margin. When you point out others' flaws you: (Check all that apply.)

- ❑ **Condemn yourself**
- ❑ **Improve your status**
- ❑ **Show contempt for God's grace**
- ❑ **Have no excuse for your own behavior**

Something is wrong with us, and it's serious. And what is most wrong with us, what we have the hardest time seeing, shows up in the way we relate. Let me illustrate.

I was talking with two committed Christian people—sincere, kind, married for 30-plus years in a solid relationship. Each reports feeling loved by the other, and both are active in their church, involved with their kids and grandkids, and co-teaching a Sunday school class on marriage.

There's just one problem. Behind the scenes, hidden from view, Gail worries if she's a good enough grandma, if her dinner guests are enjoying themselves, if the Sunday School class is being well received.

I asked Tom, Gail's husband, to share his red dot. Tom eagerly jumped into an animated discussion of the possibility of accepting a position as executive pastor of their large and still growing church. More than 20 years in the insurance business had worn him out.

While Tom went on, I noticed that Gail's gaze drifted downward, she fiddled with her hands, and she looked flat. No sparkle in her expression matched his.

I asked, "Gail, what's going on in you right now?"

"Well, I am a little uncertain. I know this means a lot to Tom, so I'm supportive, but—"

Tom interrupted. "And I'm really appreciative of Gail's support. I think she'll have more opportunities to minister, maybe together with me. I really am excited. I just want people to know Jesus, to be set free by Him."

I spoke again. "Gail, I wonder if you're feeling dismissed by Tom."

Gail looked at me. I thought I saw terror in her eyes.

"I do that a lot, don't I?" Tom's voice was softer, quiet, gentle.

She began to cry.

For the next hour we talked about Tom's loneliness, how unseen he felt. At work, he was the guy who could figure out your insurance needs and come up with a cost-effective plan to meet them. At church, he taught classes, had received lay counselor training, and talked to lots of people who appreciated his time.

"But nobody knows me. My kids don't. And Gail, well, I guess I do feel kind of known by her, but I don't know if I've ever tried to really know her. I appreciate her, I love her, we have great times together, but I don't really know her. Maybe I thought it was her job to know me or at least to accept me and to support whatever I do."

Gail warmly put her arm through his and said, "I've felt shut out for years. Just like I felt growing up. But I've never wanted to burden you with me. I've been afraid you wouldn't listen."

Now with tears in his eyes, Tom looked at me and said, "I've failed my wife. Why didn't I see it before? I really did dismiss her a few minutes ago. I didn't want to hear what she had to say."

And that's the question: Why didn't he see it before?

"Each of you should look not only to your own interests, but also to the interests of others. . . . For everyone looks out for his own interests, not those of Jesus Christ" (Phil. 2:4,21).

Read Philippians 2:4,21, printed in the margin.
Why don't we see our own relational sins?

____

Relational Sin Starts with Fear

Let me suggest something disturbing. Right now, we're all living with relational sin that we do not see. We hurt people we love and don't even know it. We think we're touching the hearts of our spouses, but we're not. We assume our friendships are close, but we're living on different planets.

Why? What's going on? What do we need to see that praying the PAPA prayer, along with good conversation, can reveal?

It starts with fear. From the time we were kids, we felt afraid. We'd keep the blankets tight around our necks so the vampire wouldn't bite us. We'd keep our hands tucked in next to our bodies, never dropping them over the side of the bed because, if we did, the alligator hiding beneath our bed would chew them off.

But our real fear was deeper. We were terrified we wouldn't measure up, no one would like us, we'd be alone. Does anyone care? Will anyone be there when I need them? Does anyone know who I am and like me? Are they strong enough to protect me? Am I alone?

No child naturally trusts God. Trust is always a supernatural activity, a work of the Spirit.

No adult fully trusts God. Complete trust is always a possibility, but it's never a reality until heaven.

"You, however, are not in the flesh, but in the Spirit, since the Spirit of God lives in you" (Rom. 8:9, HCSB).

"And we know that in all things God works for the good of those who love him, who have been called according to his purpose.... Who is he that condemns? Christ Jesus, who died—more than that, who was raised to life—is at the right hand of God and is also interceding for us" (Rom. 8:28,34).

"I sought the LORD, and he answered me; he delivered me from all my fears. Those who look to him are radiant; their faces are never covered with shame. This poor man called, and the LORD heard him; he saved him out of all his troubles. The angel of the LORD encamps around those who fear him, and he delivers them" (Ps. 34:4-7).

Read the passages from Romans 8 printed in the margin. Draw a line to connect each Person of the Trinity to the staggering truth you discover about . . .

The Holy Spirit	**He's loving you and arranging everything for your good.**
Jesus, the Son	**He's living in the very center of you right now.**
God the Father	**He's at the right hand of God, praying for you.**

We don't really believe those truths, not completely. We still live too often as if we're on our own, needing to protect ourselves.

That's relational sin. We protect ourselves from what God tells us we don't need to fear. We devote our creative energies to calm our terror, to find some way to feel alive and wanted and happy.

We all do it, in a thousand different ways. We all find a way to calm our fears, to pass ourselves off as someone whom others will want or someone whom others might find no reason to reject.

Terror goes underground. Our fear that no one could see us and want us, that our lives have no real meaning, stays hidden beneath all the ways we relate that keep us feeling pretty good.

Yet, because we haven't yet discovered the sound of our Father's voice, the one voice that can calm our deepest terror, our fears continue to drive us. We remain obsessed with ourselves, and we don't see it. We're blind to our worst faults. We do not recognize relational sin in our lives.

God often uses discerning, loving community to lead us to new levels of purging, but He always uses prayer. Relational prayer, a good conversation with our all-seeing, all-loving Papa, is essential if our purging is to run deep. Without God's wisdom and love, we'll never see our ongoing relational sin.

Why not talk with God now about your fears? Use Psalm 34:4-7, printed in the margin, to guide your conversation.

So how can we relationally pray in order to have our eyes opened to the freedom of seeing our sin and repenting, and then to release the life of God that's already in us to love others well?

Read on.

Abandon Yourself to Holiness

Pray to purge? What does that mean? How do we do it?

Praying to purge, to see what's most wrong with the way we relate, begins with a genuine openness to seeing what's wrong. And it continues with a confidence that beneath whatever is wrong is holy desire, a longing to love God and love others.

Let me suggest a simple way to come to God to be purged of sin and to release what's holy.

Ask God two questions:
1. What's wrong with the way I relate?
2. What do I want most in this relationship?

Talk to your Papa about it. Tell Him you really want Him to answer you, because you really do want to clear out anything getting in the way of your relationship with Him.

If you long to hear Papa's voice, if you want to keep close company with God, if you want to enjoy Him so much that you can feel an overwhelming desire to reveal what He's like by the way you relate with others, then it's time to abandon yourself to holiness.

We're abandoning ourselves to holiness when we come to God in prayer, wanting to see where we're wrong in the way we relate more than we want others to admit how they're wrong in the way they relate to us.

And that includes God. We can get so mad at Him for what He's allowed in our lives that, although we probably wouldn't put it this way, we're asking Him to confess His faults and repent.

We're abandoning ourselves to holiness when we come to God wanting not only to see where we're wrong but also to claim the privilege of letting others experience how God relates to them by the way we relate to them.

Let me provide a biblical background for what I'm saying. Papa told us to abandon ourselves to holiness. Through Peter, He said, "Just as he who called you is holy, so be holy in all you do" (1 Pet. 1:15). Then Peter drew on his knowledge of the Old Testament and added, "For it is written, 'Be holy, because I am holy' " (v. 16). That's a quote from Leviticus 11:44. The same words are repeated in the next verse.

What do they mean? What is God saying? If He is ordering us to work really hard at being good until we get as good as He is, we might as well quit now. Give it up. We'll never rise to that standard by trying hard to be holy.

God knows that. None of us relates perfectly. He is well aware that the greatest saints have all died flawed, that His most avid followers have further to go on their spiritual journeys than they've already come, whether they're a decade or a day away from death.

What is God telling us to do when He says, "Be holy. Be perfect. Be as good as Me"? We're already forgiven for not being holy. But how do we now get holy? God doesn't command holy action without first providing holy desire. A closer look at the passage from Leviticus will begin to make that clear.

"I am the LORD your God; consecrate yourselves and be holy, because I am holy. . . . I am the LORD who brought you up out of Egypt to be your God; therefore be holy, because I am holy" (Lev. 11:44,45).

As you read Leviticus 11:44,45, printed in the margin, circle God's commands to His children. Underline the statements that precede both commands.

Ponder the relationship between God's declaration about Himself and His commands in this passage. We'll talk more about it tomorrow.

Abandon Yourself to Holiness (Part 2)

We left off yesterday with Leviticus 11:44,45. In this passage we are told to set ourselves apart to our primary relationship. To depend on no one, not even ourselves, the way we depend on God. To set our sights on actually becoming holy, a goal we know we can't reach. To give ourselves over to the holy God who wants us (and has made it possible) to share His life. We're being told to abandon ourselves to holiness, to share in the way God relates, with radical other-centeredness, with terrible sacrifice, with humble love.

But we'll never come even close to God's example of love until we clearly understand that sin is relational. Relational sin is anything we do for the primary purpose of getting something for ourselves. It could be closing a business deal, winning a compliment, making ourselves happier, or relieving our terror of aloneness by gaining someone's friendship or affection. We might be doing these things with our advantage centrally in mind, but we're told to do all things for the glory of God.

That means the primary thought behind everything we do is to trust Him with our deepest needs and longings, to bring Him pleasure by putting all our eggs in His basket, to fix our hope for everything we hold dear on who He is and what He is doing and what He will yet do.

"The primary thought behind everything we do is to trust Him with our deepest needs and longings, to bring Him pleasure by putting all our eggs in His basket, to fix our hope for everything we hold dear on who He is and what He is doing and what He will yet do."
—Larry Crabb

Read Proverbs 3:5-6, as printed below. Cross out the incorrect words and replace them with correct words.

"Trust in the LORD with part of your heart and lean always on your own understanding; in most of your ways acknowledge Him, and you will make your paths straight."

Nothing blocks our relationship with God more effectively than relational sin. Do we wonder why He seems so far away? Why our hearts are so unsatisfied in Him? Why most of our praise to God has more to do with all the blessings we have than with the intimacy He offers?

It's relational sin. We need to pray the PAPA prayer, first to present ourselves to God, then to attend to who He is, and then to ask Him two questions: "Papa, I really want to see where I'm wrong in the way I relate to You and to my spouse and friends. Will You show me? And Papa, more than anything else, I know that way down deep I have a desire, a holy desire, to treat other people the way You treat me. Will You release that desire?"

Those for whom relational sin is not a clear category may avoid obvious sins like stealing, rape, and murder, while they unwittingly indulge in the subtle sin of protecting their own interests in relationships. And they may think they're doing nothing wrong.

When you purge yourself before Papa, when you abandon yourself to holiness, you think more of how you fall short of God's holy way of relating than of how others fail you or how badly you feel or how difficult your life may be. But your focus on your own failure does not make you hate yourself, not when you're relating to your Papa. It makes you hate your sin.

That focus doesn't leave you discouraged and feeling heavy. Broken, yes. Despairing, no. Purging lights up the path of holiness, the road paved by grace that leads into God's presence. The rhythm that carries you from presenting to attending through purging carries you toward approaching God, to enjoy the relationship with the Father you've always wanted.

"Search me, O God, and know my heart; test me and know my anxious thoughts. See if there is any offensive way in me, and lead me in the way everlasting" (Ps. 139:23-24).

Use Psalm 139:23-24, printed in the margin, to guide your prayer time as you ponder how you relate to God and to others. Use the following prayer starters; then pause and allow God to answer.

Search me God to my very depths. Show me my offensive ways so that I may correct them and relate better to others.

O Lord, in what ways are You leading me to treat others the same way You treat me?

NOTES

To the Leader:

As you reread Days 4 and 5, highlight all the explanations of what it means to abandon yourself to holiness. Prayerfully and humbly consider whether you are abandoning yourself to holiness and are committed to do so more this week.

During the Session

1. Ask: *If you were to have an intimate conversation with God, where do you envision it taking place—walking on the beach or facing each other over a cup of coffee? What do you think most believers would like to discover in an intimate conversation with God? Why do you think most believers never have that intimate conversation with God?* OR Ask participants to guess the #1 killer of both men and women in the USA. [CAD—Coronary Artery Disease, see *www.webmd.com*] Ask learners to describe the disease. [Plaque build-up blocks the arteries preventing blood flow to the heart, eventually leading to a heart attack.] Ask: *If you knew you had a blocked artery, would you do whatever was necessary to remove that blockage?* FOR EITHER OPTION Declare that the Holy Spirit lives inside of believers—He's in our hearts. Yet for many Christians something is blocking the flow of conversation with God's Spirit and the overflow of the Spirit onto others. This third step in the PAPA prayer guides us to remove anything that blocks our relationship with God.
2. Invite a volunteer to read aloud Psalm 25:8-15. Lead participants to explore what this passage reveals is involved in an intimate relationship with God. Ask: *Is it really possible to hear God speaking love and guidance to us? Then why don't we?* Complete the last activity of Day 1.
3. Ask what three things Dr. Crabb said will naturally occur when we come as we are (present) to God as He is (attend). Request someone read aloud the quotation in the margin of Day 2. Inquire: *If a relationship with God is given, then what responsibility do we have in that relationship?* State that David was willing to recognize he needed God to make this relationship work. Complete the first activity of Day 2. Ask if most people are as willing as David to recognize and acknowledge their own weaknesses and sins. Then discuss why they think this is the case. Inquire: *Why does what is most wrong with us show up in the way we relate?* Relate the illustration of Tom and Gail. Discuss the remaining two activities in Day 2.

NOTES

4. Urge the group to identify people's deepest fears. Determine how those fears lead to relational sins. Explain that in an attempt to cover up our terrors of not measuring up, belonging, or being loved, we put all our energies into deceiving ourselves and others. That deception blocks all true relationships. Instruct participants to listen for what believers should devote their energies to rather than expending energy to cover up their fears as you read aloud 1 Peter 3:14b-15 and Isaiah 8:11-13. Call for responses. Ask: *How can we know we can trust Jesus enough to focus all our energies on making Him Lord of our lives?* Use the first activity of Day 3 to help answer that question.
5. Urge participants to consider silently: *Do you long to hear God? to be intimate with Him? Do you desire to enjoy God so much that you reveal what He's like by the way you relate to others?* Declare: *If you answered yes, then you must abandon yourself to holiness.* Ask participants what they think that phrase means. [If you followed the "To the Leader" suggestion in the margin, you'll have all the explanations highlighted.] State that there is a biblical basis to the call to abandon ourselves to holiness. Discuss the final activity of Day 4.
6. Guide learners to explore the relationship between God's declarations about Himself and His commands in Leviticus 11:44-45. Declare that we are to set ourselves apart to be holy because God is a holy God who has redeemed us for the purpose of being in relationship with Him. In other words, it's all about relationship, and if we want to relate the way God relates, we must abandon ourselves to holiness. Discuss what believers would have to abandon to relate the way God relates. [We would have to abandon anything that's done for the primary purpose of getting something for ourselves.]
7. Read from Day 5 the two questions we need to ask God after we've presented ourselves to Him and attended to who He is. State that we must then be ready to confess our sins when He shows us where we've been wrong, and we must be willing to obey when He leads us to treat others like He treats us.
8. Close in prayer by reading Psalm 139:23-24.

Approach God as the "First Thing" in Your Life

You Will Hear God's Voice

Everything so far has been prelude and preparation. We are ready to approach God. Our first three steps—presenting, attending, and purging—free us to now boldly enter into our Father's presence and tell Him that we really do want to experience Him as our greatest good, as the unrivaled "first thing" in our lives who by the sheer weight of His goodness reduces every other good thing to "second-thing" status.

As you read Hebrews 4:13-16, printed in the margin, underline what happens when you present, attend, and purge yourself before God. Draw a box around words that describe how God wants you to approach Him.

Approaching God completes our new paradigm for praying, the primary purpose of which is to provide a unique opportunity to get to know Him better.

I want to be sure we are on the same page when I talk about "knowing God." So let me ask you a tough question. Do you know God? Here's an even tougher one. What does it mean to really know God?

Let me list a few phrases we hear a lot in Christian circles: knowing God, relating personally to God, enjoying God, loving God. What do people mean when they say those words? "I'm so grateful that I know God; I don't know how I'd live if I didn't." "I used to be a religious person, but now I have a personal relationship with God." "I enjoy being with God in ways I never dreamed were possible until I met Him." "I love God so much. He means everything to me." Are these just words, or do they point to something real?

Paradigm: A pattern or model.

"Nothing in all creation is hidden from God's sight. Everything is uncovered and laid bare before the eyes of him to whom we must give account. Therefore, since we have a great high priest who has gone through the heavens, Jesus the Son of God, let us hold firmly to the faith we profess. For we do not have a high priest who is unable to sympathize with our weaknesses, but we have one who has been tempted in every way, just as we are—yet was without sin. Let us then approach the throne of grace with confidence, so that we may receive mercy and find grace to help us in our time of need" (Heb. 4:13-16).

When I tell you I relate to God and enjoy Him, do I mean something different than when I speak of relating to and enjoying friends? To push the point further, are there any similarities at all between enjoying God and enjoying chocolate pie?

It's not a silly point. If I really do get more enjoyment out of pie than out of God, then an unhealthy addiction is inevitable. Whatever brings me the most joy will prove irresistible. That's just the way we're built. We were designed to enjoy joy. When nothing brings me joy, I experience despair. When something brings me joy, I go after it. That makes it important to know what is the source of real joy, joy that's deep and lasting, without bad side effects that show up years later.

Read the passages below in your Bible. Write the letter of the Scripture reference next to the statement it makes about real joy:

___ is true satisfaction in God	**a. Psalm 4:7**
___ is a gift from God	**b. Psalm 16:11**
___ results from being in God's presence	**c. Psalm 51:12**
___ accompanies salvation	**d. Psalm 90:14**

How about love? I have a pretty good idea what I mean when I say that I love my wife. But when I say that I love God, do I mean the same thing? Or is it different? And if it's different, do I mean something less or more, not as good or even better?

One measure of our love for God is whether we obey Him. But I don't love other people by obeying them. I may do what they want, but I don't think of it as obedience. Is my love for God more like driving the speed limit when I spot a cop behind me? I don't like the thought.

It seems necessary to conclude that loving God is somehow different than loving my wife or kids or friends. Loving people I experience with my five senses is not the same as loving God. It can seem less real. Relating to someone I can't see sometimes doesn't seem real at all.

But it is. Knowing God, relating to Him, enjoying Him, and loving Him is real, more real than relating to anyone else. Praying the PAPA prayer, especially approaching God, is helping me believe that. It is helping me to experience the reality of my relationship with God. But how?

Discover the Sound of God's Voice

When you learn to pray the PAPA prayer, you will discover the sound of your Father's voice. He loves a good conversation with His children. But we have to think carefully about how He speaks to us and how we speak to Him.

Does our Papa really speak? Can we really hear Him? Does He communicate with us in ways that make it possible for us to say we know Him and relate to Him and enjoy Him and love Him?

My answer is a conditional yes. I do not believe that we hear Papa's voice until we discover an empty, desolate void within us that is teeming with passionate desires for fullness. Until we cut through all the legitimate happiness and pleasure in our lives, until we look beneath every sorrow and heartache that comes from living in this world, and until we enter the deepest space in our hearts that is painfully, horribly empty, we will not discover the beautiful sound of our Father's voice. At least not as clearly as we want to.

"The key is to empty our inner space of everything but God and then to approach Him with freely acknowledged emptiness, claiming no hope of fullness unless He fills us."—Larry Crabb

God cannot see an empty heart and walk away. His love won't let Him. So the key to experiencing God is to come to Him with an empty heart. That means we'll need to get rid of everything we've already piled into the inner void that we hoped would fill it up. It's good to enjoy great kids and a beautiful sunset and an exciting vacation. It's right to feel pleasure in an intimate marriage and a meaningful job. But if all those good things (what I call "second things") have found their way into the center of our hearts, if we're using them to fill up that empty space reserved by God, for God, then we'll not hear His voice. Our claim to know Him and love Him will be shallow.

Read Philippians 3:7-11 in your Bible. What was Paul's supreme life goal? ______________________________

What did he do in his efforts to attain this goal?

____

"If you're aware that your only hope of real fullness is a relationship with God, then you're ready to go all the way with relational prayer."—Larry Crabb

The key is to empty our inner space of everything but God and then to approach Him with freely acknowledged emptiness, claiming no hope of fullness unless He fills us.

It's hard to do, for at least two reasons. First, our pride gets in the way. I'm strangely offended by having to admit I need someone else to fill me up. And second, it terrifies me. Counterfeit fullness feels pretty good. Why give up what I already have for something I'm not sure I'll get? That's scary. It requires faith. It's easier to live by sight, by self-management, by depending on things I can see, and, to some degree, control.

But they never fill me up, not completely. It may seem like they do, but it's counterfeit fullness. If you're aware that your only hope of real fullness is a relationship with God, then you're ready to go all the way with relational prayer.

"For this reason I kneel before the Father, from whom his whole family in heaven and on earth derives its name. I pray that out of his glorious riches he may strengthen you with power through his Spirit in your inner being, so that Christ may dwell in your hearts through faith. And I pray that you, being rooted and established in love, may have power, together with all the saints, to grasp how wide and long and high and deep is the love of Christ, and to know this love that surpasses knowledge—that you may be filled to the measure of all the fullness of God" (Eph. 3:14-19).

Honestly, ruthlessly, and continuously present, attend, and purge yourself in relational prayer, and I guarantee that you'll emerge from the process, again and again, feeling desperately empty. And that's good. That's your opportunity to develop a real relationship with God. Why? Because it hurts Him to see someone He loves feeling so miserable, and it pleases Him when we come to Him believing God Himself is the fullness we desire.

Papa will fill your empty heart. Discovered emptiness is our opportunity to learn what it means to know God, to relate to Him more deeply than we ever could with a terrific spouse, to enjoy Him more than chocolate pie or good friends, and to love Him with all our empty, hopeful, about-to-be-filled hearts.

Read Ephesians 3:14-19, printed in the margin. Talk to Papa. Tell Him how much you want to grasp the extent of His love for you. Tell Him how strongly you desire for Him to completely fill you so you can fully know, love, and enjoy Him.

Learning to Put First Things First

You've been praying the PAPA prayer, and your heart thumps as you read these words from Hebrews: "We can now—without hesitation—walk right up to God. … Jesus has cleared the way. … So let's do it—full of belief, confident that we're presentable inside and out" (Heb. 10:19,22, THE MESSAGE).

You read more, and your heart thumps louder. "Now that we know what we have—Jesus, this great High Priest with ready access to God—let's not let it slip through our fingers. [The writer is talking about our opportunity to know God and to get what He wants to give.] We don't have a priest who is out of touch with our reality. … [Jesus saw you crying last night; He's already told Papa about it.] So let's walk right up to him and get what he is so ready to give" (Heb. 4:14-15,16, THE MESSAGE).

So what is it? What's Papa giving? And is it what we really want?

We will receive everything we need to live the way we long to live, the way we were destined to live. We will receive everything we need to become who we truly are, not abuse victims or sex addicts or desperate housewives or incurable failures but Papa's children.

We will receive everything we need to hear His voice say, "See him? He wants Me more than anything else. See her? Look how she responds to people who treat her badly. Isn't that beautiful? She's doing it for Me. Take a look. I'm raising wonderful children."

And we'll receive the spiritual ears we need to listen as He turns to each of us, individually, and says, "You are My son. You are My daughter. I'm well pleased. I not only love you, but I like you. I enjoy your company."

Read Zephaniah 3:16-17, printed in the margin. Which of the statements describing God's actions and feelings toward you is the most meaningful to you at this point in your life?

____

"On that day they will say to Jerusalem, 'Do not fear, O Zion; do not let your hands hang limp. The LORD your God is with you, he is mighty to save. He will take great delight in you, he will quiet you with his love, he will rejoice over you with singing' " (Zeph. 3:16-17).

Briefly describe why.

____

____

____

"The power to glorify God whatever happens will be given—if you approach God, ready to receive what He's ready to give. That's a promise."—Larry Crabb

When your precious little girl lies sick in a hospital bed, what do you want the most? To see God's power heal her? Or to hear God's voice provide you with everything you need to honor Him whether she lives or dies?

If you want her healing more than you want to know God and live for His pleasure, you'll miss out on what God is ready to give. Your daughter might be healed. Of course you want that. Of course you should pray for it. That prayer, however, might not be answered. But the power to glorify God whatever happens will be given—if you approach God, ready to receive what He's ready to give. That's a promise.

Praying the PAPA prayer rearranges our values. It helps us put first things first and to keep second things in second place where they belong.

Read Luke 10:38-42 in your Bible. What desires and activities (good and bad) are distracting you right now?

____

____

What "one thing" does Jesus want to take top priority over those "many things"?

____

A Personal Example of the PAPA Prayer

Let me tell one more story of how I'm learning to pray the PAPA prayer.

It's 6:30 in the morning. I'm sitting in my bathrobe in front of the fireplace, writing these words. Earlier this morning, from 3:00 till about 4:30, I wrestled with God. I don't think I've ever experienced prayer as I just did.

I felt terrible yesterday. My head hurt. Fatigue was so extreme that eating dinner was a chore. And I felt empty, isolated, weightless. I wasn't sure what I believed about myself, life, or God. I have no idea what triggered it all. Looking back, I believe it was a spiritual battle.

When I awoke at 3:00, I felt desperate. Miserable. I had to know God better.

Read Hosea 5:15, printed in the margin. How did Larry's experience reflect the truth of this verse?

"In their misery they will earnestly seek me" (Hos. 5:15).

____

Do you more often seek God when you are: (Circle all that apply.)

Scared **Joyful** **Miserable** **Sad**

Other: ________________________________

I begged God to meet me, to let me meet Him. I thought about all that was happening in me and in my life, and I told all of it to God. I pictured Jesus the way He revealed Himself to John in Revelation. Then I made my way mentally through the books of the Bible, trying to remember how God revealed Himself and what He did in each one. I saw Him high and lifted up when I got to Isaiah, and I felt small, weak, corrupted.

I kept saying, "I'm here. I don't know what else to do. If You don't meet me, I can't make it. You're all I have. I believe You're all I need."

When I reached Hebrews 11, verse 6 appeared in my mind like a flashing billboard.

Read Hebrews 11:6 in your Bible. What must you believe if you want to draw near to God?

____

In that verse I heard my Papa's voice.

"God, I believe. Help my unbelief. Papa, I'm drawing near to You as best I know how. Please draw near to me."

At about 4:30, I stopped praying. I lay in bed till 5:00, too exhausted to get up, but no longer desperate. Like someone in a dark room standing behind you whom you can't see but whose presence you feel, Papa was there. I knew it. Jesus' words flooded into my mind: "Be of good cheer. I have overcome the world" (John 16:33, KJV). Again, that was my Papa's voice.

I felt safe, in good hands. I remember saying to myself, "I no longer feel desperate. I'm at peace. I feel hope. And joy."

But I didn't move. I wanted more sleep. Then, at 5:00, I heard a clanging noise, the sound two garbage can lids would make if they were smashed together like cymbals. The noise was muted, but it seemed to come from inside our home.

I wondered what it was, a little worried that water pipes were bursting or something had fallen. But I didn't move. I wanted more sleep. I heard the noise again. When the sound came a third time, I got up.

The sound stopped. I didn't hear it again. I knew its source. The Spirit was telling me to get my tired body out of bed and write this chapter. I know that sounds weird, strange, fantastic. But if God wants to make noise like garbage can lids banging together, I guess He can. I had been trying to write for six days. Nothing came. Just 40 or 50 pages of paper filled with scribbles that meant nothing, made no sense.

"I'm flowing through you. I'm giving you the chapter. Get up and write." Again, Papa was speaking to me through His Spirit.

I was still tired. I wanted more sleep. But I wanted to get up. I didn't shower or brush my teeth. I couldn't wait to get my pad of paper and pen.

The Story Continues

Dressed in my bathrobe, I came downstairs, poured a little grape juice into a glass, broke a piece of bread from a loaf, and knelt before the fireplace. I read from 1 Corinthians 11.

Read 1 Corinthians 11:23-26 in your Bible.
What do you re-enact every time you partake of the Lord's Supper? ______________________

I read on. "If you give no thought (or worse, don't care) about the broken body of the Master when you eat and drink, you're running the risk of serious consequences" (v. 29, THE MESSAGE).

As I knelt, with the bread and juice on the hearth in front of me, I trembled. Do I care that Jesus died? Do I care more that my daughter-in-law's pregnancy goes well, that the weather cooperates with my golf plans, that my neck pain goes away, that everyone in our family stays healthy?

Examine yourself and answer the following question honestly: Do you care that Jesus died?

- ❑ **Honestly, no. His death has nothing to do with my life.**
- ❑ **I guess so. But I don't think about it much.**
- ❑ **Usually. But sometimes I get caught up in myself.**
- ❑ **Absolutely. It's why I live and breathe.**

Like a gentle thunderbolt, the thought struck me: I couldn't have approached God as my Papa for the last several hours if Jesus hadn't died. I'd be stuck looking for relief from my emotional pain some other way, scrambling to feel better for reasons that couldn't amount to much.

But because Jesus died and rose, my Judge is now my Papa. I have a Guide and a Healer. God is now my King and my Friend. And I have God's

If you enjoyed these studies from Larry Crabb and desire to purchase your own copy of *The PAPA Prayer* to read and study in greater detail, visit the LifeWay Christian Store serving you. Or you can order a copy by calling 1-800-233-1123.

life in me. He's my donor as well. I'm in the royal family. And, as I observe the remembrance, I can confidently ask Him to stir the life that's in me and pour it out of me, through my words as I write for the next couple of hours. That was Papa's voice.

I ate the bread and drank the juice. I didn't tremble. I didn't cry. I smiled. It's all true! The bottom line is good. I can walk right up to God, the same God who divided the Red Sea and raised Jesus from the dead, and get what He wants to give me.

And I can pick up my pen and tell you all about it. That's when I decided to end this study on a personal note, to tell you how God used the PAPA prayer to carry me from despair to joy.

The joy is real. The despair is gone, though not completely. Joy that comes from the Spirit never eliminates pain; it takes its place at the center. Until heaven. Then it fills everything, every place, every relationship.

For now, I still groan. Life is not what I want it to be. I'm not who I want to be. But right now I know that I'm loved, I'm accepted; God is not discarding me, He's preparing me; I'm wanted and I matter; I have the weightiness of one who is called to be part of the most important thing going on in the world today.

Nothing can change that. But we don't always see it. We don't always know it. Sometimes we don't see it at all. Sometimes we wonder if it's really true.

That's where I was yesterday afternoon and evening. That's where I was when I woke up at 3:00 this morning. That's where I'll be again, and again and again till I get home.

But now, this moment, it's not where I am. I'm filled with joy. And hope. And peace. I know it's possible to feel this way in the middle of difficult emotions. It's the fruit of the Spirit.

And it's what your Papa wants to give you, no matter what is happening in your life. Come to Him to receive what He's eager to give. Come empty. Come with your desires. Come believing. Learn to pray the PAPA prayer. You'll discover the sound of your Father's voice.

Read Psalm 63 in your Bible. Empty yourself before God, acknowledging that the desert you are in has left you dry and faint. Then pray this psalm to God, expressing your eager desire to know Him intimately.

NOTES

To the Leader:

Pray Ephesians 3:14-19 for each participant in your class, inserting each person's name in place of the word "you" as you voice your prayer to God.

Before the Session

1. Secure a copy of *The Message* to read during the lesson.
2. Briefly familiarize yourself with the next study coming in *MasterWork.*

During the Session

1. Ask: *If you were to physically approach God on His throne, what would be going on inside you? How would you handle yourself physically? What would you say?* OR Organize the class into three groups. Assign one of the following scenarios to each group and ask them to describe how they would approach that authority and why: 1. The principal's office when they were a child; 2. The boss's office to ask for a raise; 3. The Oval Office to meet with the President. Suggest they consider whether they would approach confidently, angrily, sassily, fearfully, apathetically. Allow groups to share. Ask how most people approach God and why.
2. Discuss the first activity of Day 1. Ask why we can approach God confidently even though we are totally bare before Him [Hint: see Heb. 4:14-15.] Evaluate how the PAPA prayer has been a paradigm shift for the class. Read this sentence from Day 1: "Approaching God completes our new paradigm." Ask: *What do many people believe is the primary purpose for praying? Why would this new way of praying actually result in more answered prayers than the "asking God" way?* Remind participants of your study of John 15 in Week 1—when you abide in Christ and know Him fully, then you ask for what He already wants to give. Examine what participants think it means to really know God. Explore how enjoying and loving God may be different than enjoying and loving earthly things.
3. Read the questions in the second paragraph of Day 2. Inquire: *Why did Dr. Crabb answer those questions with a conditional yes? What did he say is the key to experiencing God and why? What, then, is our responsibility for hearing our Father's voice?* Discuss the first activity of Day 2. Direct participants to state from Philippians 3:4-6,13 what Paul had to empty himself of before he could fully experience God. Determine how

NOTES

Philippians 3:7-11 helps the class further understand what it means to know God. Explain that when we fully know God we are so completely identified with Him that our former life is dead and He is our first thing. Inquire: *Why is it so hard to approach God completely empty? When are you ready to go all the way with relational prayer?* [When you become aware that your only hope of fullness is a relationship with God.] *Why is it a good thing to feel desperately empty?*

4. Read Hebrews 10:19-22. State: *When you approach someone completely empty and needy, you make yourself completely vulnerable to all manner of hurts. So why can we trust God with our empty, needy selves? What will we receive when we approach Him with confidence?* [Everything we need to become who we were created to be.] *What will we hear God say as we approach Him confidently with empty hearts in hand?* Allow volunteers to share their responses to the first activity of Day 3. Explore how the PAPA prayer rearranges our values. Discuss the final activity of Day 3—assure participants they can give general, rather than personal, responses to the first question.
5. Remind participants that Dr. Crabb invited us to join him on his personal journey in learning to pray in a more meaningful way. He concluded this study with a personal illustration of how he's learning to pray the PAPA prayer. Relate his story from Day 4, discussing the learning activities at the appropriate points in the story. Invite volunteers to share about a time they clearly heard God's voice when they were miserable and worn down.
6. Continue with Dr. Crabb's story from Day 5, explaining that he felt led to share a Lord's Supper service just between himself and God. Discuss the first activity of Day 5. Read 1 Corinthians 11:29 from *The Message.* Request participants silently consider the second activity. Ask: *Why do we need to care that Jesus died? How do we demonstrate with our lives that we care?* Continue relaying Dr. Crabb's story of how God carried him from despair to joy because he took the time to present himself honestly to God, attend to how he thought about God, purge himself of anything that blocked his relationship with God, and then approached God with confidence. Read aloud the final two paragraphs of Day 5. Invite volunteers to share how this study has helped them hear God better.
7. Introduce the new study beginning next week. Close in prayer.